NON SANZ DROICT.

William Shakespeare

THE MERCHANT
OF VENICE

With New Dramatic Criticism
and an Updated Bibliography

EDITED BY KENNETH MYRICK

The Signet Classic Shakespeare
GENERAL EDITOR: SYLVAN BARNET

A SIGNET CLASSIC

SIGNET CLASSIC
Published by the Penguin Group
Penguin Books USA Inc., 375 Hudson Street,
New York, New York 10014, U.S.A.
Penguin Books Ltd, 27 Wrights Lane,
London W8 5TZ, England
Penguin Books Australia Ltd, Ringwood,
Victoria, Australia
Penguin Books Canada Ltd, 10 Alcorn Avenue,
Toronto, Ontario, Canada M4V 3B2
Penguin Books (N.Z.) Ltd, 182–190 Wairau Road,
Auckland 10, New Zealand

Penguin Books Ltd, Registered Offices:
Harmondsworth, Middlesex, England

Published by Signet Classic, an imprint of New American Library,
a division of Penguin Books USA Inc.

First Signet Classic Printing, February, 1965
31   30   29   28   27   26   25   24   23

 REGISTERED TRADEMARK—MARCA REGISTRADA

Library of Congress Catalog Card Number: 86-62300

Printed in the United States of America

Contents

Shakespeare: Prefatory Remarks

Between the record of his baptism in Stratford on 26 April 1564 and the record of his burial in Stratford on 25 April 1616, some forty documents name Shakespeare, and many others name his parents, his children, and his grandchildren. More facts are known about William Shakespeare than about any other playwright of the period except Ben Jonson. The facts should, however, be distinguished from the legends. The latter, inevitably more engaging and better known, tell us that the Stratford boy killed a calf in high style, poached deer and rabbits, and was forced to flee to London, where he held horses outside a playhouse. These traditions are only traditions; they may be true, but no evidence supports them, and it is well to stick to the facts.

Mary Arden, the dramatist's mother, was the daughter of a substantial landowner; about 1557 she married John Shakespeare, who was a glove-maker and trader in various farm commodities. In 1557 John Shakespeare was a member of the Council (the governing body of Stratford), in 1558 a constable of the borough, in 1561 one of the two town chamberlains, in 1565 an alderman (entitling him to the appellation "Mr."), in 1568 high bailiff—the town's highest political office, equivalent to mayor. After 1577, for an unknown reason he drops out of local politics. The birthday of William Shakespeare, the eldest son of this locally prominent man, is unrecorded; but the Stratford parish register records that the infant was baptized on 26 April 1564. (It is quite possible that he was born on 23

April, but this date has probably been assigned by tradition because it is the date on which, fifty-two years later, he died.) The attendance records of the Stratford grammar school of the period are not extant, but it is reasonable to assume that the son of a local official attended the school and received substantial training in Latin. The masters of the school from Shakespeare's seventh to fifteenth years held Oxford degrees; the Elizabethan curriculum excluded mathematics and the natural sciences but taught a good deal of Latin rhetoric, logic, and literature. On 27 November 1582 a marriage license was issued to Shakespeare and Anne Hathaway, eight years his senior. The couple had a child in May, 1583. Perhaps the marriage was necessary, but perhaps the couple had earlier engaged in a formal "troth plight" which would render their children legitimate even if no further ceremony were performed. In 1585 Anne Hathaway bore Shakespeare twins.

That Shakespeare was born is excellent; that he married and had children is pleasant; but that we know nothing about his departure from Stratford to London, or about the beginning of his theatrical career, is lamentable and must be admitted. We would gladly sacrifice details about his children's baptism for details about his earliest days on the stage. Perhaps the poaching episode is true (but it is first reported almost a century after Shakespeare's death), or perhaps he first left Stratford to be a schoolteacher, as another tradition holds; perhaps he was moved by

> Such wind as scatters young men through the world,
> To seek their fortunes further than at home
> Where small experience grows.

In 1592, thanks to the cantankerousness of Robert Greene, a rival playwright and a pamphleteer, we have our first reference, a snarling one, to Shakespeare as an actor and playwright. Greene warns those of his own educated friends who wrote for the theater against an actor who has presumed to turn playwright:

There is an upstart crow, beautified with our feathers,

that with his *tiger's heart wrapped in a player's hide*
supposes he is as well able to bombast out a blank verse
as the best of you, and being an absolute Johannes-
factotum is in his own conceit the only Shake-scene in
a country.

The reference to the player, as well as the allusion to
Aesop's crow (who strutted in borrowed plumage, as an
actor struts in fine words not his own), makes it clear that
by this date Shakespeare had both acted and written. That
Shakespeare is meant is indicated not only by "Shake-
scene" but by the parody of a line from one of Shakespeare's plays, *3 Henry VI:* "O, tiger's heart wrapped in
a woman's hide." If Shakespeare in 1592 was prominent
enough to be attacked by an envious dramatist, he probably had served an apprenticeship in the theater for at
least a few years.

In any case, by 1592 Shakespeare had acted and written, and there are a number of subsequent references to
him as an actor: documents indicate that in 1598 he is a
"principal comedian," in 1603 a "principal tragedian," in
1608 he is one of the "men players." The profession of
actor was not for a gentleman, and it occasionally drew
the scorn of university men who resented writing speeches
for persons less educated than themselves, but it was respectable enough: players, if prosperous, were in effect
members of the bourgeoisie, and there is nothing to suggest that Stratford considered William Shakespeare less
than a solid citizen. When, in 1596, the Shakespeares were
granted a coat of arms, the grant was made to Shakespeare's father, but probably William Shakespeare (who
the next year bought the second-largest house in town)
had arranged the matter on his own behalf. In subsequent
transactions he is occasionally styled a gentleman.

Although in 1593 and 1594 Shakespeare published two
narrative poems dedicated to the Earl of Southampton,
Venus and Adonis and *The Rape of Lucrece,* and may
well have written most or all of his sonnets in the middle
nineties, Shakespeare's literary activity seems to have been
almost entirely devoted to the theater. (It may be significant that the two narrative poems were written in years

when the plague closed the theaters for several months.) In 1594 he was a charter member of a theatrical company called the Chamberlain's Men (which in 1603 changed its name to the King's Men); until he retired to Stratford (about 1611, apparently), he was with this remarkably stable company. From 1599 the company acted primarily at the Globe Theatre, in which Shakespeare held a one-tenth interest. Other Elizabethan dramatists are known to have acted, but no other is known also to have been entitled to a share in the profits of the playhouse.

Shakespeare's first eight published plays did not have his name on them, but this is not remarkable; the most popular play of the sixteenth century, Thomas Kyd's *The Spanish Tragedy*, went through many editions without naming Kyd, and Kyd's authorship is known only because a book on the profession of acting happens to quote (and attribute to Kyd) some lines on the interest of Roman emperors in the drama. What is remarkable is that after 1598 Shakespeare's name commonly appears on printed plays—some of which are not his. Another indication of his popularity comes from Francis Meres, author of *Palladis Tamia: Wit's Treasury* (1598): in this anthology of snippets accompanied by an essay on literature, many playwrights are mentioned, but Shakespeare's name occurs more often than any other, and Shakespeare is the only playwright whose plays are listed.

From his acting, playwriting, and share in a theater, Shakespeare seems to have made considerable money. He put it to work, making substantial investments in Stratford real estate. When he made his will (less than a month before he died), he sought to leave his property intact to his descendants. Of small bequests to relatives and to friends (including three actors, Richard Burbage, John Heminges, and Henry Condell), that to his wife of the second-best bed has provoked the most comment; perhaps it was the bed the couple had slept in, the best being reserved for visitors. In any case, had Shakespeare not excepted it, the bed would have gone (with the rest of his household possessions) to his daughter and her husband. On 25 April 1616 he was buried within the chancel of the church at Stratford. An unattractive monument to his memory, placed on a wall near the grave, says he died on 23 April. Over the grave itself are the lines, perhaps by Shakespeare, that (more than his literary fame) have kept his bones undisturbed in the crowded burial ground where old bones were often dislodged to make way for new:

> Good friend, for Jesus' sake forbear
> To dig the dust enclosèd here.
> Blessed be the man that spares these stones
> And cursed be he that moves my bones.

Thirty-seven plays, as well as some nondramatic poems, are held to constitute the Shakespeare canon. The dates of composition of most of the works are highly uncertain, but there is often evidence of a *terminus a quo* (starting point) and/or a *terminus ad quem* (terminal point) that provides a framework for intelligent guessing. For example, *Richard II* cannot be earlier than 1595, the publication date of some material to which it is indebted; *The Merchant of Venice* cannot be later than 1598, the year Francis Meres mentioned it. Sometimes arguments for a date hang on an alleged topical allusion, such as the lines about the unseasonable weather in *A Midsummer Night's Dream,* II.i.81–117, but such an allusion (if indeed it is an allusion) can be variously interpreted, and in any case there is always the possibility that a topical allusion was inserted during a revision, years after the composition of a play. Dates are often attributed on the basis of style, and although conjectures about style usually rest on other conjectures, sooner or later one must rely on one's literary sense. There is no real proof, for example, that *Othello* is not as early as *Romeo and Juliet,* but one feels *Othello* is later, and because the first record of its performance is 1604, one is glad enough to set its composition at that date and not push it back into Shakespeare's early years. The following chronology, then, is as much indebted to informed guesswork and sensitivity as it is to fact. The dates, necessarily imprecise, indicate something like a scholarly consensus.

PLAYS

1588–93	*The Comedy of Errors*
1588–94	*Love's Labor's Lost*
1590–91	*2 Henry VI*
1590–91	*3 Henry VI*
1591–92	*1 Henry VI*
1592–93	*Richard III*
1592–94	*Titus Andronicus*
1593–94	*The Taming of the Shrew*
1593–95	*The Two Gentlemen of Verona*
1594–96	*Romeo and Juliet*
1595	*Richard II*
1594–96	*A Midsummer Night's Dream*
1596–97	*King John*
1596–97	*The Merchant of Venice*
1597	*1 Henry IV*
1597–98	*2 Henry IV*
1598–99	*Henry V*
1598–1600	*Much Ado About Nothing*
1599	*Julius Caesar*
1599–1600	*As You Like It*
1599–1600	*Twelfth Night*
1600–01	*Hamlet*
1597–1601	*The Merry Wives of Windsor*
1601–02	*Troilus and Cressida*
1602–04	*All's Well That Ends Well*
1603–04	*Othello*
1604	*Measure for Measure*
1605–06	*King Lear*
1605–06	*Macbeth*
1606–07	*Antony and Cleopatra*
1605–08	*Timon of Athens*
1607–09	*Coriolanus*
1608–09	*Pericles*
1609–10	*Cymbeline*
1610–11	*The Winter's Tale*
1611	*The Tempest*
1612–13	*Henry VIII*

POEMS

1592	*Venus and Adonis*
1593–94	*The Rape of Lucrece*
1593–1600	*Sonnets*
1600–01	*The Phoenix and the Turtle*

Shakespeare's Theater

In Shakespeare's infancy, Elizabethan actors performed wherever they could—in great halls, at court, in the courtyards of inns. The innyards must have made rather unsatisfactory theaters: on some days they were unavailable because carters bringing goods to London used them as depots; when available, they had to be rented from the innkeeper; perhaps most important, London inns were subject to the Common Council of London, which was not well disposed toward theatricals. In 1574 the Common Council required that plays and playing places in London be licensed. It asserted that

> sundry great disorders and inconveniences have been found to ensue to this city by the inordinate haunting of great multitudes of people, specially youth, to plays, interludes, and shows, namely occasion of frays and quarrels, evil practices of incontinency in great inns having chambers and secret places adjoining to their open stages and galleries,

and ordered that innkeepers who wished licenses to hold performances put up a bond and make contributions to the poor.

The requirement that plays and innyard theaters be licensed, along with the other drawbacks of playing at inns, probably drove James Burbage (a carpenter-turned-actor) to rent in 1576 a plot of land northeast of the city walls and to build here—on property outside the jurisdiction of the city—England's first permanent construction designed for plays. He called it simply the Theatre. About all that is known of its construction is that it was wood. It soon had imitators, the most famous being the Globe

(1599), built across the Thames (again outside the city's jurisdiction), out of timbers of the Theatre, which had been dismantled when Burbage's lease ran out.

There are three important sources of information about the structure of Elizabethan playhouses—drawings, a contract, and stage directions in plays. Of drawings, only the so-called De Witt drawing (c. 1596) of the Swan—really a friend's copy of De Witt's drawing—is of much significance. It shows a building of three tiers, with a stage jutting from a wall into the yard or center of the building. The tiers are roofed, and part of the stage is covered by a roof that projects from the rear and is supported at its front on two posts, but the groundlings, who paid a penny to stand in front of the stage, were exposed to the sky. (Performances in such a playhouse were held only in the daytime; artificial illumination was not used.) At the rear of the stage are two doors; above the stage is a gallery. The second major source of information, the contract for the Fortune, specifies that although the Globe is to be the model, the Fortune is to be square, eighty feet outside and fifty-five inside. The stage is to be forty-three feet broad, and is to extend into the middle of the yard (i.e., it is twenty-seven and a half feet deep). For patrons willing to pay more than the general admission charged of the groundlings, there were to be three galleries provided with seats. From the third chief source, stage directions, one learns that entrance to the stage was by doors, presumably spaced widely apart at the rear ("Enter one citizen at one door, and another at the other"), and that in addition to the platform stage there was occasionally some sort of curtained booth or alcove allowing for "discovery" scenes, and some sort of playing space "aloft" or "above" to represent (for example) the top of a city's walls or a room above the street. Doubtless each theater had its own peculiarities, but perhaps we can talk about a "typical" Elizabethan theater if we realize that no theater need exactly have fit the description, just as no father is the typical father with 3.7 children. This hypothetical theater is wooden, round or polygonal (in *Henry V* Shakespeare calls it a "wooden *O*"), capable of holding some eight hundred spectators standing in the yard around the projecting elevated stage and some fifteen hundred additional spectators seated in the three roofed galleries. The stage, protected by a "shadow" or "heavens" or roof, is entered by two doors; behind the doors is the "tiring house" (attiring house, i.e., dressing room), and above the doors is some sort of gallery that may sometimes hold spectators but that can be used (for example) as the bedroom from which Romeo—according to a stage direction in one text—"goeth down." Some evidence suggests that a throne can be lowered onto the platform stage, perhaps from the "shadow"; certainly characters can descend from the stage through a trap or traps into the cellar or "hell." Sometimes this space beneath the platform accommodates a sound-effects man or musician (in *Antony and Cleopatra* "music of the hautboys is under the stage") or an actor (in *Hamlet* the "Ghost cries under the stage"). Most characters simply walk on and off, but because there is no curtain in front of the platform, corpses will have to be carried off (Hamlet must lug Polonius' guts into the neighbor room), or will have to fall at the rear, where the curtain on the alcove or booth can be drawn to conceal them.

Such may have been the so-called "public theater." Another kind of theater, called the "private theater" because its much greater admission charge limited its audience to the wealthy or the prodigal, must be briefly mentioned. The private theater was basically a large room, entirely roofed and therefore artificially illuminated, with a stage at one end. In 1576 one such theater was established in Blackfriars, a Dominican priory in London that had been suppressed in 1538 and confiscated by the Crown and thus was not under the city's jurisdiction. All the actors in the Blackfriars theater were boys about eight to thirteen years old (in the public theaters similar boys played female parts; a boy Lady Macbeth played to a man Macbeth). This private theater had a precarious existence, and ceased operations in 1584. In 1596 James Burbage, who had already made theatrical history by building the Theatre, began to construct a second Blackfriars theater. He died in 1597, and for several years this second Blackfriars theater was used by a troupe of boys, but in 1608 two of Burbage's sons and five other actors (including Shakespeare) became joint operators of the theater, using it in the winter when the open-air Globe was unsuitable. Perhaps such a smaller theater, roofed, artificially illuminated, and with a tradition of a courtly audience, exerted an influence on Shakespeare's late plays.

Performances in the private theaters may well have had intermissions during which music was played, but in the public theaters the action was probably uninterrupted, flowing from scene to scene almost without a break. Actors would enter, speak, exit, and others would immediately enter and establish (if necessary) the new locale by a few properties and by words and gestures. Here are some samples of Shakespeare's scene painting:

> This is Illyria, lady.

> Well, this is the Forest of Arden.

> This castle hath a pleasant seat; the air
> Nimbly and sweetly recommends itself
> Unto our gentle senses.

On the other hand, it is a mistake to conceive of the Elizabethan stage as bare. Although Shakespeare's Chorus in *Henry V* calls the stage an "unworthy scaffold" and urges the spectators to "eke out our performance with your mind," there was considerable spectacle. The last act of *Macbeth*, for example, has five stage directions calling for "drum and colors," and another sort of appeal to the eye is indicated by the stage direction "Enter Macduff, with Macbeth's head." Some scenery and properties may have been substantial; doubtless a throne was used, and in one play of the period we encounter this direction: "Hector takes up a great piece of rock and casts at Ajax, who tears up a young tree by the roots and assails Hector." The matter is of some importance, and will be glanced at again in the next section.

The Texts of Shakespeare

Though eighteen of his plays were published during his lifetime, Shakespeare seems never to have supervised their publication. There is nothing unusual here; when a playwright sold a play to a theatrical company he surrendered his ownership of it. Normally a company would not publish the play, because to publish it meant to allow competitors to acquire the piece. Some plays, however, did get published: apparently treacherous actors sometimes pieced together a play for a publisher, sometimes a company in need of money sold a play, and sometimes a company allowed a play to be published that no longer drew audiences. That Shakespeare did not concern himself with publication, then, is scarcely remarkable; of his contemporaries only Ben Jonson carefully supervised the publication of his own plays. In 1623, seven years after Shakespeare's death, John Heminges and Henry Condell (two senior members of Shakespeare's company, who had performed with him for about twenty years) collected his plays—published and unpublished—into a large volume, commonly called the First Folio. (A folio is a volume consisting of sheets that have been folded once, each sheet thus making two leaves, or four pages. The eighteen plays published during Shakespeare's lifetime had been issued one play per volume in small books called quartos. Each sheet in a quarto has been folded twice, making four leaves, or eight pages.) The First Folio contains thirty-six plays; a thirty-seventh, *Pericles,* though not in the Folio, is regarded as canonical. Heminges and Condell suggest in an address "To the great variety of readers" that the republished plays are presented in better form than in the quartos: "Before you were abused with diverse stolen and surreptitious copies, maimed and deformed by the frauds and stealths of injurious impostors that exposed them; even those, are now offered to your view cured and perfect of their limbs, and all the rest absolute in their numbers, as he [i.e., Shakespeare] conceived them."

Whoever was assigned to prepare the texts for publication in the First Folio seems to have taken his job seriously and yet not to have performed it with uniform care. The sources of the texts seem to have been, in general, good unpublished copies or the best published copies. The first play in the collection, *The Tempest,* is divided into acts and scenes, has unusually full stage directions and descriptions of spectacle, and concludes with a list of the characters, but the editor was not able (or willing) to present all of the succeeding texts so fully dressed. Later texts occasionally show signs of carelessness: in one scene of *Much Ado About Nothing* the names of actors, instead of characters, appear as speech prefixes, as they had in the quarto, which the Folio reprints; proofreading throughout the Folio is spotty and apparently was done without reference to the printer's copy; the pagination of *Hamlet* jumps from 156 to 257.

A modern editor of Shakespeare must first select his copy; no problem if the play exists only in the Folio, but a considerable problem if the relationship between a quarto and the Folio—or an early quarto and a later one —is unclear. When an editor has chosen what seems to him to be the most authoritative text or texts for his copy, he has not done with making decisions. First of all, he must reckon with Elizabethan spelling. If he is not producing a facsimile, he probably modernizes it, but ought he to preserve the old form of words that apparently were pronounced quite unlike their modern forms—"lanthorn" "alablaster"? If he preserves these forms, is he really preserving Shakespeare's forms or perhaps those of a compositor in the printing house? What is one to do when one finds "lanthorn" and "lantern" in adjacent lines? (The editors of this series in general, but not invariably, assume that words should be spelled in their modern form.) Elizabethan punctuation, too, presents problems. For example in the First Folio, the only text for the play, Macbeth rejects his wife's idea that he can wash the blood from his hand:

> no: this my Hand will rather
> The multitudinous Seas incarnardine,
> Making the Greene one, Red.

Obviously an editor will remove the superfluous capitals, and he will probably alter the spelling to "incarnadine," but will he leave the comma before "red," letting Macbeth speak of the sea as "the green one," or will he (like most modern editors) remove the comma and thus have Macbeth say that his hand will make the ocean *uniformly* red?

An editor will sometimes have to change more than spelling or punctuation. Macbeth says to his wife:

> I dare do all that may become a man,
> Who dares no more, is none.

For two centuries editors have agreed that the second line is unsatisfactory, and have emended "no" to "do": "Who dares do more is none." But when in the same play Ross says that fearful persons

> floate vpon a wilde and violent Sea
> Each way, and moue,

need "move" be emended to "none," as it often is, on the hunch that the compositor misread the manuscript? The editors of the Signet Classic Shakespeare have restrained themselves from making abundant emendations. In their minds they hear Dr. Johnson on the dangers of emending: "I have adopted the Roman sentiment, that it is more honorable to save a citizen than to kill an enemy." Some departures (in addition to spelling, punctuation, and lineation) from the copy text have of course been made, but the original readings are listed in a note following the play, so that the reader can evaluate them for himself.

The editors of the Signet Classic Shakespeare, following tradition, have added line numbers and in many cases act and scene divisions as well as indications of locale at the beginning of scenes. The Folio divided most of the plays into acts and some into scenes. Early eighteenth-century editors increased the divisions. These divisions, which provide a convenient way of referring to passages in the plays, have been retained, but when not in the text chosen as the basis for the Signet Classic text they are

enclosed in square brackets [ ] to indicate that they are
editorial additions. Similarly, although no play of Shakespeare's published during his lifetime was equipped with
indications of locale at the heads of scene divisions, locales
have here been added in square brackets for the conven-
ience of the reader, who lacks the information afforded
to spectators by costumes, properties, and gestures. The
spectator can tell at a glance he is in the throne room,
but without an editorial indication the reader may be
puzzled for a while. It should be mentioned, incidentally,
that there are a few authentic stage directions—perhaps
Shakespeare's, perhaps a prompter's—that suggest locales;
for example, "Enter Brutus in his orchard," and "They
go up into the Senate house." It is hoped that the brack-
eted additions provide the reader with the sort of help
provided in these two authentic directions, but it is equally
hoped that the reader will remember that the stage was
not loaded with scenery.

No editor during the course of his work can fail to recol-
lect some words Heminges and Condell prefixed to the
Folio:

> It had been a thing, we confess, worthy to have been
> wished, that the author himself had lived to have set
> forth and overseen his own writings. But since it hath
> been ordained otherwise, and he by death departed
> from that right, we pray you do not envy his friends
> the office of their care and pain to have collected and
> published them.

Nor can an editor, after he has done his best, forget Heminges and Condell's final words: "And so we leave you to
other of his friends, whom if you need can be your guides.
If you need them not, you can lead yourselves, and others.
And such readers we wish him."

SYLVAN BARNET
Tufts University

Introduction

The Merchant of Venice is the earliest of three superb comedies in which Shakespeare has set a generous and clear-sighted woman in sharp contrast to a no less unusual, but markedly unsocial man. From beginning to end, Portia and Shylock—like Rosalind and Jaques in *As You Like It* and Viola and Malvolio in *Twelfth Night*—remain poles apart. It is significant that Portia in her greatest scene, and the two other heroines in nearly all of their scenes, are disguised as men. Only the audience and one confidante share their secret. Knowing it, the spectators naturally tend to center their interest in them and to view the play through their eyes. Portia, Rosalind, and Viola tend to overshadow their lovers, not because, as is often asserted, the men are not worthy of them, but because of their fascinating double roles.

Their respective opponents—Shylock, Jaques, and Malvolio—are all vivid, but strange and isolated figures. None is an actual villain, but each has been accurately called an *anti-hero*.

On the Elizabethan stage, it was probably easier for Portia to take the leading role than it is in the modern theater. In Shakespeare's company there was a better balance than in modern times, when the star actor tends to overshadow all the others. The lady's handicap is especially formidable when the star is, like Sir Henry Irving, both the manager of the theater and even the director of the troupe. Ellen Terry was at her best, she said, when she played against Irving, but she could not be the central figure of the play that Portia is meant to be. At times in the nineteenth century, Shylock so overshadowed everyone else that the beautiful final act was omitted entirely.

It is pretty clear today that when Jaques or Malvolio is allowed to usurp the leading role, the entire play is thrown out of balance. In *The Merchant of Venice* the problem is complicated by other factors. The late E. E. Stoll, in a justly famous essay, argued that Shylock was always an unsympathetic figure to the Elizabethans because he is a miser, a usurer, and a Jew. The attitude of the civilized world has changed toward all three. We have hardly ever known a miser. The usurer seems only a man who lends money at interest. And prejudice against Jews is hateful to all fair-minded people. How then can any decent person appreciate this comedy in the spirit in which Stoll thought it was written? How valid is his view?

The strength of Stoll's interpretation lies in his strong common sense, massive erudition, and insights into dramatic method. He stressed the great importance of the common beliefs, prejudices, and superstitions that distinguish Shakespeare's time from our own era. He emphasized the significance of our vivid first impressions, of the contrasts of character with character and plot with subplot, and the necessity of approaching a play as a play and not as a book. He saw that as readers we tend to respond as individuals, but as spectators we tend to catch the contagion of the crowd and respond like everyone else. With all his gifts as an interpreter of Shakespeare, however, Stoll appears sometimes to have been strangely insensitive to the humanizing ideals of Shakespeare's age and the poetic atmosphere of his plays.

"The Merchant of Venice is a fairy tale," declared that wise man of the theater, Harley Granville-Barker. We may think he made too much of this point, but he reminded us forcibly that the play is set in the realm of high romance. We cannot understand it in terms of modern realism. Strange and wonderful are the stories of the caskets, the pound of flesh, and the beautiful girl disguised as a wise young judge—not to mention the miser's daughter who blossoms into a delightful and virtuous lady, filled with the joy of life. We begin to sense this poetic atmosphere in the very first scene.

ACT I

i. Antonio and Bassanio

Antonio is not in the least the stodgy, smug, intolerant businessman that he is often supposed to be. A great merchant prince of the fabulous city of Venice, he sends out his splendid ships as far as Mexico and the Indies and shares his wealth with the needy and oppressed. In his quiet way, he—like Bassanio and Portia, Lorenzo and Jessica—is a figure of romance. His friends see poetry in his commercial ventures:

> Your argosies with portly sail—
> Like signiors and rich burghers on the flood,
> Or as it were the pageants of the sea—
> Do overpeer the petty traffickers
> That cursy to them, do them reverence,
> As they fly by them with their woven wings.

His friends see also a great and ever-present danger. The modern merchant is often depicted as a type enjoying comfortable security. Salerio and Solanio, like people to-day when they think of the astronauts, are fascinated and appalled by the risks that Antonio takes. Yet he faces these constant dangers with a quiet mind. Shakespeare, like the medieval poets, could find romance in the old themes of love and battle; but with a poet's insight into men and affairs, he discovered it also in the merchant-adventurer's commerce, in which, as in knightly times, danger went hand in hand with beauty and high achievement.

Antonio is admired and beloved for his good deeds. Yet the poet has wisely given him a relatively passive role. If we felt his emotions too keenly, the scene of his trial would be too painful for comedy. His "sadness" contributes to this passiveness. One guess about the cause of his melancholy is that he fears Bassanio's approaching marriage will separate him from his friend. Another is that he is just in a strange mood. Antonio, however, is too generous to regret his friend's happy marriage, and the emphasis given to his mood suggests an important meaning.

We can find it in one of the common ideas of the Elizabethan age, the belief in presentiments. Shakespeare uses it in many plays to foreshadow future events, especially dangers and misfortunes. It is somewhat analogous to the faith in extrasensory perception, which (though not shared by the present editor) is held by some of our very intelligent contemporaries. A striking parallel to Antonio's sadness is in *Richard II,* which was probably written just before *The Merchant of Venice.* In one scene the Queen's attendants are troubled about her sadness, a much more violent melancholy than Antonio's. Suddenly, after only a few moments, she hears the shocking news of Bolingbroke's rebellion, which is to bring about the dethronement and murder of her husband. She instantly recognizes the meaning of her presentiment.

Antonio's unaccountable sadness is a less violent experience than the Queen's, apparently because the danger is more remote and because in the end he escapes it. But in kind, though not in degree, the two presentiments are alike.

Few moderns have such faith in extrasensory perception as many intelligent Elizabethans had in presentiments. Therefore, we go astray if we invent rationalistic explanations for Antonio's sadness which neither the poet nor his audience had in mind—just as we do when we explain Banquo's ghost, or King Hamlet's, as a figment of the imagination. These are cases that require the "willing suspension of disbelief."

Antonio's presentiment has an important dramatic function. It suggests to the audience some great danger of which he and his friends are totally unconscious. Thus it creates dramatic irony, quickens suspense, and awakens a warm concern for this modest and generous merchant prince, who is so much admired and beloved. In his next scene it also heightens our concern for him when he readily agrees to Shylock's apparently jovial suggestion that Antonio forfeit a pound of flesh if the three thousand ducats are not paid back on time.

Bassanio has sometimes been misunderstood even more

seriously than Antonio—as a contemptible man of fashion who puts his friend's life in danger so that he can gamble on winning an heiress. His best qualities, as Professor Bernard Grebanier has remarked, have become increasingly rare in the last century and a half. He speaks with "an elegance which is innate and unconscious. . . . The miraculous thing is that . . . this patrician quality of the mind is united . . . with a manliness, an unaggressive virility of a kind to which the twentieth century is becoming totally a stranger." His first words about Portia,

> In Belmont is a lady richly left,

do not mean that he wants to marry her for money, but that "there is good reason to promise the return of the loan" he is asking of his friend. His eloquent words about Portia herself assure us that his love for her is genuine.

As the play develops, we find Bassanio's friend, Gratiano, asking to go with him to Belmont. A loud extrovert, Gratiano "speaks an infinite deal of nothing," and is the last person Bassanio would choose to accompany him on a delicate mission. But with a few very frank words of caution, he generously accedes to his friend's surprising request, without the slightest trace of irritation. At Belmont we see Bassanio not only as a delightful gentleman, but as a man of thought and insight as he meditates on which casket to choose. When he has won Portia, we like him for his overwhelming joy, his modesty, and his entire devotion to her.

The world of Bassanio and Antonio is not ours. Its values are chiefly those of a governing class—courage, justice, a high sense of honor, courtesy, learning, a love of beauty, compassion, and humility. Lord Bassanio has the highest rank of anyone in the play except the Duke, yet he never shows even a trace of arrogance. Like Sir Philip Sidney, the most admired and beloved young Englishman of Shakespeare's time, Bassanio has lived beyond his means because of the position he occupies. For him, as for Sidney and Castiglione, life is at once an earnest task, an adventure, and a fine art. To Sidney, Shakespeare, and their contemporaries, the marriage of so fine a nobleman as Bassanio with a virtuous, gifted, humanely educated, and wholly delightful lady of wealth would be altogether fitting.

ii. Portia

As for Portia, even most of Shylock's warmest partisans commonly find her irresistible in her early scenes, however they may dislike her way of defeating him in the court scene. Some, of course, grumble at her deft satire of her egregious parcel of wooers, and one critic can declare solemnly, "Portia herself, for some reason, is the least lovable of Shakespeare's comedy heroines." Harley Granville-Barker, who saw nearly all the characters with remarkable clarity, observed that the poet reveals Portia's character "to us mainly in little things, and lets us feel its whole happy virtue in the melody of her speech." Granville-Barker also points out that, hedged about as she is by her father's will in the early scenes, there is very little for her to do. However this may be, the strangeness of her situation captures our attention, and the naturalness of her thoughts and feelings leads us to identify ourselves at once with her cause and to sense the irony of her situation. Although her father did not trust her to choose a husband for herself, yet, as her shrewd comments on her suitors reveal, few women ever had a keener insight into men's characters than she. Nevertheless, she does not really rebel against her father's will, and when she learns it has driven away six unwelcome suitors, she is amazed and delighted at the old man's foresight. Her filial piety meant more to the Elizabethans than to us, but her quick feelings, her sense of responsibility, her wit and keen perception of the ridiculous belong to every age and make her one of the most magnetic of heroines.

iii. Shylock and Antonio

  Shylock. Three thousand ducats—well.
  Bassanio. Ay, sir, for three months.
  Shylock. For three months—well.

Shylock comes before us abruptly, with no previous hint that he exists. Antonio and Portia, in their first speeches, confide their thoughts and feelings to their friends. Bassanio, alone with Antonio, pours out his heart. But Shylock, from the first words he utters, is a strangely isolated figure, secretive and calculating. We begin to discover his real thoughts only when he utters them aside as Antonio enters. The hatred that he expresses so vehemently and his efforts later in the scene to appear as Antonio's cordial friend are in glaring contradiction.

Defenders of Shylock often argue that at first his offer of friendship is sincere, and that he never meant the forfeit of a pound of Antonio's flesh as anything but "a merry jest," until Jessica deserted him to elope with one of Antonio's Christian friends. This interpretation ignores the basic principle that every essential point must be clear to the simplest groundling. When a character in Shakespeare speaks aside to the audience, he always speaks his real thoughts. When Shylock says, as Antonio enters,

> If I can catch him once upon the hip,
> I will feed fat the ancient grudge I bear him,

we have no choice but to believe him.

E. E. Stoll's famous, though one-sided, interpretation of Shylock is indispensable for an understanding of Shylock's real character. Stoll demonstrates that the issue between the Jewish moneylender and the Christian merchant is not simply the taking of interest. It is the usurer's merciless exploitation of his victims. He is no mere "banker," as H. B. Charlton called him, but a crafty and ruthless loan shark. The Tudor laws against usury stated an ideal and then compromised with the practical facts of trade. They outlawed any interest on any loan but imposed no penalty if the rate did not exceed ten percent (nearly twice the rate commonly charged today for a mortgage loan). The typical usurer, however, found devious ways of exacting far more than the law allowed. His special victims were the inexperienced and the very needy—widows and orphans, and young gentlemen not yet possessed of their inheritance. For an original loan of a

hundred pounds, the clever usurer might gain in a few
years real estate worth five hundred or a thousand pounds,
bringing his wretched debtor to beggary or death. The
Elizabethan hatred of usury was sanctioned by Aristotle's
theory that money cannot breed money; but far more important were the enormous interest rates and fraudulent
contracts of clever scoundrels. Recognizing Shylock as a
usurer, the Elizabethans must have been hostile to him,
especially when they saw him plotting against Antonio's
life.

Why does he hate this generous merchant? Antonio has
denounced Shylock in public. He has loaned money to
the usurer's victims, has charged them no interest at all
and thus enabled many of them to escape total ruin. Although he has never till now either charged interest on
a loan, or paid it, Antonio is ready to "break a custom"
rather than have his best friend risk losing Portia. For
this, many critics, supposing the issue to involve one of
Antonio's absolute principles, charge him with hypocrisy.
But Antonio, as a man of affairs, is less interested in
theory than in results. The charge would be valid only if
he were exacting interest from a debtor. To rescue the
usurer's victims, he has loaned them money at no interest.
To enable Bassanio to win Portia, he will himself pay
interest on a loan, rather than let his best friend lose his
dearest hopes. In each case his concern is to bring generous aid to those in need.

While discussing the loan with Antonio, Shylock suddenly digresses and pours out one of his most eloquent
and moving speeches. In the Rialto, he declares, in full
view of crowds of merchants, Antonio has publicly disgraced him. He has called him dog, kicked him, and spat
upon him. Some very intelligent readers have refused to
believe these charges, but Antonio himself confirms them.

> I am as like to call thee so again,
> To spet on thee again, to spurn thee too.

It is a strange and shameful fact that for many centuries Christians held it to be proper to spit in a Jew's
face on certain occasions. The idea goes back to the

Crucifixion, when the Jews mocked Christ and spat upon him. Similarly, the horrible idea that the Jews had become a race accursed by God arose from their refusal to accept Jesus as the Messiah. In spite of these bitter prejudices, however, it is hard to believe that Shakespeare approved Antonio's way of publicly denouncing the usurer. The words he gives Shylock seem designed to show us how it feels to be an outcast in a Christian society.

It is hard to know the exact meaning of a gesture common four centuries ago. Just what did it mean in the social context of Elizabethan England? The great Queen herself once "spat upon a courtier's cloak that displeased her." The act of thumbing the nose was originally an obscene insult, but we have seen friends use it as a bit of light teasing.

As a compassionate man, outraged by the usurer's inhumanity to his victims, Antonio is capable of hot indignation, as we see in his answer to Shylock's charge. Today he might expose a dangerous public enemy in a newspaper article or radio address, or by presenting the facts to the prosecuting attorney. In Shakespeare's Venice, where the practice of usury seems to have been as inhuman as anywhere else, Antonio takes the kind of direct action that decent Americans sometimes took against an unscrupulous man in pioneer days on the frontier. Antonio deliberately insults the usurer, literally kicks him out of his place of business, does all he can to turn public opinion against him, and spends his own money to rescue Shylock's victims. Christ himself, though he preached the gospel of love, denounced the oppressors and hypocrites in public and whipped the money changers out of the temple. Antonio's just indignation is natural and understandable, and so is Shylock's bitter resentment. We begin to see Shylock as his own worst enemy, poisoned by greed and hate.

ACTS II AND III

From the harsh but strangely compelling figure of the anti-hero, we turn immediately to Portia. In her scenes with Morocco and Aragon, she is a marvel of self-control

and courtesy, although some of her speeches to them are
edged with an irony that they never catch. Her whole future
happiness is at stake, for neither Morocco nor Aragon can
appreciate the best qualities of a Renaissance lady. Morocco is a warm-hearted man of honor and courage, who has
the grace to think he may not deserve her. But there is
something naïve, almost barbaric, in his desire that his
fate be decided by having his rivals and himself cut their
flesh to see whose blood is reddest. His mind is very simple;
hers is highly endowed by nature and has acquired the best
culture of a remarkable age and country. We wish Morocco
well, but he is no mate for Portia. As for Aragon, he has the
presumptuous pride that the Elizabethans disliked in the
Spaniards. He has also the naïveté to suppose that a man
could actually deserve such a woman as Portia, and that he
is that man. Most of Shakespeare's genuine lovers are, like
Portia and Bassanio, humbled by their love.

One key to the meaning of a Shakespeare play is the way
he directs our sympathies. In many of his masterpieces
there is one person, or more, through whose eyes we are
particularly invited to see the other characters and the
events. In *Henry the Fourth* it is chiefly Prince Hal, in
Hamlet it is Horatio and Hamlet, in *Twelfth Night* it is
Viola. Who is it in *The Merchant of Venice?*

In the opening scene, in which Antonio is the center of
attention but at first does little, we see him as four of his
friends do. In Shylock's first scene, many modern readers
see him as he sees himself, but those who realize what a
usurer actually was will look at him as Bassanio and Antonio do. Stoll, in a long analysis, argued that whenever we
begin to sympathize with Shylock, his greed and hatred are
emphasized. He accuses Antonio of disgracing him and
then plots to kill him. He speaks of Launcelot as a kind
patch, but adds that he is "a huge feeder." He speaks kindly
to his daughter as "Jessica, my girl," and instantly remem-
bers his dream of moneybags. In one of his greatest scenes,
he pours out a passionate defense of the Jewish people and
a challenge to Christians to practice the mercy and humility
that they profess; but he ends the speech on the note of
revenge, arranging with Tubal to meet him at the synagogue

to plan the legalized murder of a generous Christian merchant.

Stoll makes an important point. But we can turn it around and show, on his own evidence, that in each of Shylock's scenes, except the briefest, he wins the sympathy of the audience for at least a few moments. When do we ever see the least touch of kindly feeling in Iago or Goneril? Shylock differs, too, from other Shakespearean villains— from Angelo in *Measure for Measure,* with whom he is often compared, and from Hamlet's uncle, King Claudius —in that these men are entirely conscious of their villainy. At the trial, Shylock can ask, apparently in all sincerity, "What judgment shall I dread, doing no wrong?" The unique thing about Shylock is this strange sincerity. He can nurse the most diabolical passions and imagine he does no wrong.

Doubtless the Elizabethans laughed with Solanio and Salerio when they baited Shylock, for as Stoll has emphasized, a general audience in the theater will respond to the mood of the characters on stage. Yet we must never suppose that these two friends of Antonio express more than a very small part of Shakespeare's attitude toward the Jew. These characters can scarcely be distinguished from one another, and we do not go to such people to find Shakespeare's whole meaning. Their function is chiefly to release the feelings of the audience or to tell us news. In the court scene, the jeers and imprecations of Gratiano provide a similar release. But "Gratiano speaks an infinite deal of nothing, more than any man in all Venice." The shallow comments of this excited extrovert contrast with the wisdom of Portia and the considered judgment of Antonio.

Throughout the play, Shakespeare has invited us to look at the other characters and the action through Portia's eyes, and to share her sympathies. One way he does this is in the skilful arrangement of contrasting scenes. He places Shylock's first scene between Portia's first and second, and her third just after Jessica's flight. Beginning with Portia's fourth scene (II.ix), he alternates her scenes with Shylock's with almost exact regularity until their encounter in the courtroom. In this way the poet silently draws ever more sharply the contrast between the usurer and the wise Renaissance lady, before either has any idea of the other's existence.

Our sympathies are never so strongly with Portia, or with Bassanio, as in the beautiful scene where he wins her, particularly in the tense moments while she watches him meditating on which casket to choose, and in the climax that brings them a happiness they can hardly express. When the sudden news comes of Antonio's catastrophic losses, Portia instantly offers her entire fortune to save her husband's friend of whom until now she has never heard. Like Bassanio and Antonio, she knows how to "give and hazard all she hath." In this scene of love and generous friendship, we see Portia at her best.

In the next scene we find Shylock at his worst, raging madly at Antonio and promising to take his life. It is his one scene in the play in which we can have no spark of sympathy for him. Is destiny on his side, or on Portia's?

SHYLOCK AND JUDAISM

As we approach the court scene, we must face the question of Shakespeare's attitude toward the Jews. Stoll and some others believed he shared the hateful prejudice that had disgraced Christianity for over fifteen centuries. In 1935, Professor John W. Draper sharply challenged this view. "Shylock the Jew was merely exotic local color," he declared. "Shylock the usurer was a commentary on London life." The second statement is certainly true; there were many usurers in the great city, and their cruelty was notorious. The first statement is partly true. Dr. J. L. Cardozo seems to have proved that—contrary to common opinion—there were no Jews, or almost none, dwelling anywhere in Shakespeare's London, unless we except the small band of a few hundred Portuguese who had converted from Judaism to Christianity. Shylock must have been an exotic figure to the Elizabethans.

His Judaism, however, is emphasized again and again. In Shylock the great virtues of the ancient Hebrews have often been corrupted into the nearest vices. Reverence for law has degenerated into legalism, loyalty to his own people into a vehement antipathy to Christians, practical sagacity into the love of money, a noble love of justice into a fanatical thirst for a revenge that excludes every thought of mercy. Yet until the climax of the court scene, Shylock is blindly unconscious of doing anything wrong. Here is no mere comic butt, no mere hypocrite and villain, but a warped and dangerous fanatic—sometimes comic, sometimes hateful—impervious to any normal appeal to common sense or natural kindness, but always strangely human. Something has poisoned this man, and apparently a whole people, originally splendidly endowed by nature.

Most modern readers find the source of the poison in Christian persecution. Shakespeare touches on this idea, especially in Shylock's great defense of the humanity of the Jews. But his emphasis lies elsewhere. Shylock is fiercely conscious of his "sacred nation." He defends the iniquitous practice of usury by citing the Old Testament. As Christians had always said of the Jews from the days of St. Paul, he insists on the bare letter of the law and ignores the spirit. He goes to the synagogue to plan Antonio's death. In the court scene he declares solemnly he has "an oath in heaven" that he will cut the pound of flesh from Antonio. Earlier we see momentarily a better side of his Judaism, in his memory of his wife's first gift. It is obvious, nevertheless, that Shakespeare has many times connected Shylock's worst qualities with the Hebrew religion.

So hateful is this idea to us that we must be very certain just what it meant to Shakespeare. The prejudice is not at all the Nazi's hatred of the Jew's blood and supposed race, for Jessica is "a daughter to his blood" but not to "his manners," i.e., his moral values and actions. The hostility is directed against Shylock's code of ethics and the religion that is assumed to be its source.

How could the humane and clear-sighted Shakespeare ever have taken such a view of one of the world's great religions? Perhaps we can most easily understand his view if we remember the attitude toward Puritans that is held today by some humane but not well-informed people. Without examining the facts with an open mind, they see the Puritans as narrow zealots or even hypocrites, who—like

Shylock—despised beauty and merrymaking, loved money, and looked down with contempt on their less sanctified neighbors. Although these people think of themselves as enlightened and tolerant, they regard the Puritan religion as a fanaticism—a perverted view of life which warped a man's mind, chilled his sympathies, and poisoned his relations with all who did not share the special outlook of the chosen few. There is some truth in this picture, but impartial historians know it to be, on the whole, distorted and unjust.

The analogy with Judaism is very close, for the Puritans' emphasis on the Old Testament made them the most Hebraic of Christian groups. In Elizabeth's reign, even men of large minds and generous sympathies could regard the Jewish faith very much as many of our contemporaries regard Puritanism. For centuries Christians had been taught almost universally that the ancient religion of Israel had degenerated into a narrow fanaticism, teaching a pedantic adherence to the mere letter of the law and ignoring the spirit. "The letter killeth but the spirit giveth life," wrote St. Paul. As a Christian scholar of our time, James Parkes, wrote: "The inadequacy of the law . . . was [the Church Fathers'] continual accusation against the Jews." Parkes also observed that our English word "law" is no adequate equivalent for the original word "Torah" in the Hebrew text:

> The written law was . . . the basis of Torah, but Torah itself was the complete revelation of the holy community or nation through which the individual in every act could fulfill the purpose of God in his creation.

Between this lofty Hebrew concept and the Christian idea of the divine mercy which at once fulfills and transcends the law, there is no irreconcilable conflict. Shakespeare and the members of his audience, however, could not know what scholars so wise as Richard Hooker (1554?–1600) had not discovered.

The modern parallel to Shylock is not the Jews. It is the Nazi persecutors of the Jews.

THE TRIAL

The scene of Antonio's trial surpasses almost anything Shakespeare had ever written previously in both range and power. The sustained clash of wills, the battle of ideas, the variety of characterization, the prolonged suspense (relieved now and then by touches of comedy), the deepening irony, and the stunning reversal of fortune when Portia finally turns Shylock's own weapon against himself—all these reveal the hand of a great craftsman and the inspiration of a master poet.

Often in the nineteenth century, and sometimes in the twentieth, this scene has been interpreted as "The Tragedy of Shylock." Stoll interpreted it as harsh comedy. After the reversal of fortune, he says, "The Jew's very words are echoed by Portia and Gratiano as they jeer, and at every turn that justice takes . . . there are now peals and shouts of laughter." Neither interpretation does justice to Shakespeare's sane and compassionate view.

In the first place, though everyone else is appalled at Shylock's cruelty, he himself is here a figure of real dignity. The mad fierceness of his last two scenes is gone. As he addresses the Duke, his language is eloquent, and his strange reasoning is cogent. Confident in the justice of his cause, he regards Gratiano's bitter curse with amused indifference. To the Duke and Portia he shows a courteous respect. Up to the sudden reversal of his fortunes, he treats her with admiration and genuine friendliness. In one sense, we see him at his best in this scene. With some exceptions, his bearing in more than half the scene is that of a civilized man of affairs. The contrast between his manner and his fanatical purpose heightens the effect. He is a shrewd and persuasive advocate in his astounding case. When the Duke makes a powerful appeal that he show "human gentleness and love," Shylock defends with powerful logic his right to take Antonio's life.

Duke. How shalt thou hope for mercy, rend'ring none?
Shylock. What judgment shall I dread, doing no wrong?

The tension of the scene mounts steadily, but Shake-speare skillfully breaks it now and then. Just before Bel-lario's messenger (Nerissa) comes in, we are deeply moved by the selfless friendship of Bassanio and Antonio, as each insists that he should die for the other. Then the sight of Nerissa trying, without quite perfect success, to act the part of an experienced law clerk brings a hint of comedy. As spectators we need not laugh, but all will feel a slight lessening of tension. When Shylock takes the occasion to whet his knife on his sole, the grotesque act brings us still nearer to comedy.

Portia enters dressed as a judge and gets quickly down to business. Shylock's procedure cannot be attacked under the law.

> Then must the Jew be merciful.
> On what compulsion must I?

The question reveals how tightly his moral code is bound to the letter of the law. What it forbids he will never do. But he can neither give nor forgive. Portia, in a speech that almost sums up the meaning of the play, explains that mercy must be an entirely free gift. It blesses the giver and the receiver alike. To show mercy is the privilege of kings, of God himself. But if Shylock insists on the letter of the law, sentence must be given against the merchant. Then comes Portia's quiet masterstroke.

> Tarry a little; there is something else.
> This bond doth give thee here no jot of blood.

Stunned as he is, Shylock tries to accept the previous offer of thrice the bond. But having refused it, he now has no claim on it or even on the bare principal. The law has yet another hold on him. He, an alien, has plotted against a citizen's life. All his vast wealth is forfeit, half to Antonio, half to the state, and his life lies "in the mercy of the Duke only."

Portia has appealed in vain to reason, to charity, and to self-interest. Now she has turned the letter of the law against Shylock. He has been guilty of the mad presumption that the Greeks called *hubris.* For him this sudden blow is a profound psychological shock. No longer can he boast he does no wrong. *By his own code,* the letter of the law, he knows he is guilty of a deadly crime. Stunned and broken, he kneels before the Duke.

The strict court of Venice understands mercy as well as justice. Justice demands that the offender be punished, be forced to make amends to the injured party, and be restrained from doing further harm. Mercy draws a distinction between a crime willed and a crime enacted. As the prince of Christian humanists, Erasmus, says of charity, mercy requires that the Christian "be an enemy only to vice. Let him kill the Turk, but save the man." Let Portia and the Duke kill his fanaticism, but save the man.

Can we honestly say that he receives mercy? By the mere letter of the law he receives it abundantly. He now owns not a penny's worth of property, and his life is forfeit. The Duke instantly pardons him his life, but Shylock is ready to die. It is now Antonio's opportunity to show mercy. Under the law, one half of Shylock's wealth is now Antonio's, the other half the state's. Following a hint of the Duke's, the merchant proposes, first, that the half which is the state's be restored conditionally to Shylock. Second, he offers to use his own half as a permanent loan without interest, and at the Jew's death to give it outright to Jessica and Lorenzo. He imposes two conditions: first, that the young couple shall receive all Shylock's property at his death; second, that he immediately become a Christian.

In view of Shylock's own cruelty to his luckless debtors, these terms would seem to us both just and merciful, were it not for the forced conversion. This we are bound to resent if we think of the Hebrew faith only as it really is. But if we see it as it had been misunderstood by Christians for over fifteen centuries, we can describe it in the words of Edmund Burke (written with no reference to Judaism) as "an uncouth, pernicious, and degrading superstition." As we painfully rediscovered in Hitler's Germany, the perversion of the instincts of religion and human loyalty can be one of the most dangerous forces in the world. The fanatical Nazis had to be reeducated before they could ever be trusted; so Shylock, too, must give up his fanatical adherence to the letter of the law. It is noteworthy that Antonio, the Duke, and Portia never show any hatred of Shylock. In their view he is being saved from himself. Shakespeare's information about a great religious faith was defective and largely mistaken, but his own values are universal.

FULFILLMENT

The final scene at Portia's estate will seem irrelevant and bitterly ironical to those who still regard Shylock as a victim of Christian bigotry. To others it will be something very different. A good man has been saved from death. A dangerous but greatly gifted man has begun to see life in an altogether new way. Now, in the peace and the magical beauty of the evening, Lorenzo and Jessica are recalling famous lovers of the past. Their earnest mood, broken by playful teasing, Lorenzo's poetic nature as revealed in his words about the music of the spheres, the entrance of Portia and Nerissa, happy in a work of redemption fully achieved—all this suggests powerfully the happy harmony of life at its best. Gratiano's sudden quarrel with Nerissa and the women's harmless teasing of the men about the rings they gave away bring us back to ordinary life and to the mood of comedy. Portia's news that three of Antonio's argosies

> Are richly come to harbor suddenly,

and her good news also for Jessica and Lorenzo give promise of long happiness for them. Gratiano's final speech brings a laugh from the audience.

To those who can see Shylock as neither an entire villain nor a hero, but a gifted man whose fanatical hatred makes him his own worst enemy until he is saved from himself, *The Merchant of Venice* is no tragedy. To those who can view the play from the point of view of the wise, realistic, and compassionate heroine, it is one of Shakespeare's most beautiful and most significant comedies.

KENNETH MYRICK
Tufts University

The Merchant of Venice

[*Dramatis Personae*

The Duke of Venice
The Prince of Morocco } suitors to Portia
The Prince of Aragon
Antonio, a merchant of Venice
Bassanio, his friend, suitor to Portia
Gratiano
Salerio   } friends to Antonio and Bassanio
Solanio
Lorenzo, in love with Jessica
Shylock, a Jew
Tubal, a Jew, his friend
Launcelot Gobbo, a clown, servant to Shylock
Old Gobbo, father to Launcelot
Leonardo, servant to Bassanio
Balthasar } servants to Portia
Stephano
Portia, an heiress
Nerissa, her waiting woman
Jessica, daughter to Shylock
Magnificoes of Venice, Officers of the court of justice,
    Jailer, Servants, and other Attendants

Scene: Venice and Belmont]

The Merchant of Venice

[ACT I

Scene I. *Venice. A street.*]

Enter Antonio, Salerio, and Solanio.

Antonio. In sooth I know not why I am so sad.°[1]
   It wearies me, you say it wearies you;
   But how I caught it, found it, or came by it,
   What stuff 'tis made of, whereof it is born,
   I am to learn;°   5
   And such a want-wit° sadness° makes of me
   That I have much ado to know myself.

Salerio. Your mind is tossing on the ocean,°
   There where your argosies° with portly° sail—
   Like signiors and rich burghers on the flood,   10
   Or as it were the pageants° of the sea—
   Do overpeer the petty traffickers
   That cursy° to them, do them reverence,
   As they fly by them with their woven wings.

Solanio. Believe me, sir, had I such venture° forth,   15
   The better part of my affections would

---

[1] The degree sign (°) indicates a footnote, which is keyed to the text by line number. Text references are printed in boldface type; the annotation follows in roman type.
I.i.1. **sad** sober, depressed   **5 am to learn** need to learn, cannot guess (the incomplete line indicates a short pause)   **6 want-wit** dull fellow   **6 sadness** depression   **8 ocean** (pronounced "ó-ce-an")   **9 argosies** great merchant ships   **9 portly** stately   **11 pageants** floats, splendidly decorated wagons in the shape of castles, dragons, etc.   **13 cursy** curtsy, bow   **15 venture** unpredictable enterprise

Be with my hopes abroad. I should be still°
Plucking the grass to know where sits the wind,
Peering in maps for ports and piers and roads;°
And every object that might make me fear
Misfortune to my ventures, out of doubt
Would make me sad.

Salerio.   My wind cooling my broth
Would blow me to an ague° when I thought
What harm a wind too great might do at sea.
I should not see the sandy hourglass run
But I should think of shallows and of flats,
And see my wealthy *Andrew*° docked in sand,
Vailing° her high top lower than her ribs
To kiss her burial. Should I go to church
And see the holy edifice of stone
And not bethink me straight of dangerous rocks,
Which touching but my gentle° vessel's side
Would scatter all her spices on the stream,
Enrobe the roaring waters with my silks—
And in a word, but even now worth this,°
And now worth nothing?° Shall I have the thought
To think on this, and shall I lack the thought
That such a thing bechanced° would make me sad?
But tell not me! I know Antonio
Is sad to think upon his merchandise.

Antonio. Believe me, no. I thank my fortune for it,
My ventures are not in one bottom° trusted,
Nor to one place; nor is my whole estate
Upon the fortune of this present year.
Therefore my merchandise makes me not sad.

Solanio. Why then you are in love.

Antonio.   Fie, fie!

Solanio. Not in love neither? Then let us say you are sad

17 still always   19 roads harbors   23 ague trembling fit   27 Andrew the name of a ship   28 Vailing lowering, in recognition of a
superior   32 gentle noble and gentle; hence, splendid and frail
35, 36 this, nothing (spoken with an emphatic gesture)   38 be-
chanced should it happen   42 bottom ship

Because you are not merry; and 'twere as easy
For you to laugh and leap, and say you are merry
Because you are not sad. Now by two-headed Janus,°   50
Nature hath framed strange° fellows in her time:
Some that will evermore peep through their eyes
And laugh like parrots at a bagpiper,
And other of such vinegar aspect
That they'll not show their teeth in way of smile   55
Though Nestor° swear the jest be laughable.

Enter Bassanio, Lorenzo, and Gratiano.

Here comes Bassanio, your most noble kinsman,
Gratiano, and Lorenzo. Fare ye well;
We leave you now with better company.

Salerio. I would have stayed till I had made you merry,   60
If worthier friends had not prevented° me.

Antonio. Your worth is very dear in my regard.
I take it your own business calls on you,
And you embrace th' occasion to depart.

Salerio. Good morrow, my good lords.   65

Bassanio. Good signiors both, when shall we laugh? Say, when?
You grow exceeding strange;° must it be so?

Salerio. We'll make our leisures to attend on yours.
        Exeunt Salerio and Solanio.

Lorenzo. My Lord Bassanio, since you have found Antonio,
We two will leave you; but at dinner time   70
I pray you have in mind where we must meet.

Bassanio. I will not fail you.

Gratiano. You look not well, Signior Antonio.

50 **two-headed Janus** Roman god of entrances and hence of all beginnings; depicted with two faces, one cheerful, one sad, symbolizing the uncertainty of the future (Solanio suggests that Antonio is as strange a figure as Janus)   51 **strange** marvelously queer   56 **Nestor** the oldest and most venerable Greek leader in the Trojan War; a type of gravity and wisdom   61 **prevented** forestalled   67 **strange** distant

You have too much respect upon° the world;
75 They lose it that do buy it with much care.
Believe me, you are marvelously changed.

Antonio. I hold the world but as the world, Gratiano—
A stage, where every man must play a part,
And mine a sad one.

Gratiano.   Let me play the fool!
80 With mirth and laughter let old wrinkles come,
And let my liver° rather heat with wine
Than my heart cool with mortifying groans.°
Why should a man whose blood is warm within
Sit like his grandsire, cut in alabaster?
85 Sleep when he wakes? And creep into the jaundice°
By being peevish? I tell thee what, Antonio—
I love thee, and 'tis my love that speaks—
There are a sort of men whose visages
Do cream and mantle° like a standing pond,
90 And do a willful stillness entertain°
With purpose to be dressed in an opinion°
Of wisdom, gravity, profound conceit,°
As who should say, "I am Sir Oracle,°
And when I ope my lips, let no dog bark!"
95 O my Antonio, I do know of these
That therefore only are reputed wise
For saying nothing; when I am very sure
If they should speak, would almost dam° those ears,
Which hearing them would call their brothers fools.
100 I'll tell thee more of this another time.

74 respect upon regard for   81 liver one of the supposed seats of the
passions   82 mortifying groans groans supposed to deaden vitality
(by drawing blood from the heart)   85 jaundice disease thought to
be caused by peevishness   89 cream and mantle become impassive
like thick cream on a bowl of milk, or a mantle of scum on a pond
90 entertain assume   91 opinion reputation (as in line 102)   92 profound conceit power of forming profound conceptions   93 I am Sir
Oracle i.e., I am as wise as a Greek oracle (inspired by the gods)
98 dam (often emended to "damn," and probably a pun: If these
silent and reputedly wise men ever did speak, the abundance of their
foolish words would not only dam up the ears of the listeners, but
also make the listeners call the formerly silent men fools, and thus
bring on the listeners the penalty of damnation which is pronounced
on all who apply this term to a brother-man. See Matthew 5:22)

But fish not with this melancholy bait
For this fool gudgeon,° this opinion.
Come, good Lorenzo. Fare ye well awhile;
I'll end my exhortation after dinner.

Lorenzo. Well, we will leave you then till dinner time. *105*
I must be one of these same dumb wise men,
For Gratiano never lets me speak.

Gratiano. Well, keep me company but two years moe,°
Thou shalt not know the sound of thine own tongue.

Antonio. Fare you well; I'll grow a talker for this gear.° *110*

Gratiano. Thanks i' faith; for silence is only commendable
In a neat's tongue° dried and a maid not vendible.°
                    Exeunt [*Gratiano and Lorenzo*].

Antonio. Is that anything now?

Bassanio. Gratiano speaks an infinite deal of nothing,
more than any man in all Venice. His reasons are as *115*
two grains of wheat hid in two bushels of chaff: you
shall seek all day ere you find them, and when you
have them they are not worth the search.

Antonio. Well, tell me now, what lady is the same
To whom you swore a secret pilgrimage *120*
That you today promised to tell me of?

Bassanio. 'Tis not unknown to you, Antonio,
How much I have disabled mine estate,
By something° showing a more swelling port°
Than my faint means would grant continuance.° *125*
Nor do I now make moan to be abridged°

101-02 **But . . . gudgeon** don't cultivate melancholy to gain a reputation for silent wisdom, for the judgment of the multitude is stupid
("gudgeon" = proverbially foolish fish)   108 **moe** more ("moe" is
the old positive form of which "more" was the comparative)   110
gear stuff (a mild jest, showing that Gratiano has cheered Antonio
for a moment)   112 **neat's tongue** beef tongue   112 **vendible** sal-
able, i.e., marriageable   124 **something** somewhat   124 **swelling
port** impressive style of living   125 **grant continuance** allow me
to continue   126 **abridged** cut down

From such a noble rate;° but my chief care
Is to come fairly off from the great debts
Wherein my time, something too prodigal,°
130 Hath left me gaged.° To you, Antonio,
I owe the most in money and in love,
And from your love I have a warranty
To unburden all my plots and purposes
How to get clear of all the debts I owe.

135 *Antonio.* I pray you, good Bassanio, let me know it,
And if it stand as you yourself still° do,
Within the eye of honor, be assured
My purse, my person, my extremest means
Lie all unlocked to your occasions.°

140 *Bassanio.* In my schooldays, when I had lost one shaft°
I shot his fellow° of the selfsame flight°
The selfsame way, with more advisèd° watch,
To find the other forth; and by adventuring both
I oft found both. I urge this childhood proof°
145 Because what follows is pure innocence.°
I owe you much, and like a willful youth°
That which I owe is lost; but if you please
To shoot another arrow that self way
Which you did shoot the first, I do not doubt,
150 As I will watch the aim, or° to find both,
Or bring your latter hazard° back again
And thankfully rest debtor for the first.

Antonio. You know me well, and herein spend but time
To wind about my love with circumstance;°
155 And out of doubt you do me now more wrong
In making question of my uttermost

---

127 rate scale   129 my time, something too prodigal the lavish way
I spent my time   130 gaged pledged   136 still always   139 occasions needs   140 shaft arrow   141 fellow duplicate   141 selfsame
flight identical in size and in the feathers   142 advisèd considered
144 proof experience   145 pure innocence childlike sincerity   146
like a willful youth i.e., like one who neglected sound advice and
learned by making mistakes   150 or either   151 hazard thing risked
154 To wind . . . circumstance to approach my love circuitously with
elaborate talk

Than if you had made waste of all I have.
Then do but say to me what I should do
That in your knowledge may by me be done,
And I am prest unto it.° Therefore speak.   160

Bassanio. In Belmont is a lady richly left;°
And she is fair and, fairer than that word,
Of wondrous virtues.° Sometimes from her eyes
I did receive fair speechless messages.
Her name is Portia, nothing undervalued   165
To° Cato's daughter, Brutus' Portia;°
Nor is the wide world ignorant of her worth,
For the four winds blow in from every coast
Renownèd suitors, and her sunny locks
Hang on her temples like a golden fleece,   170
Which makes her seat° of Belmont Colchos' strond,°
And many Jasons come in quest of her.
O my Antonio, had I but the means
To hold a rival place with one of them,
I have a mind presages me° such thrift°   175
That I should questionless be fortunate!

Antonio. Thou know'st that all my fortunes are at sea;
Neither have I money, nor commodity°
To raise a present sum. Therefore go forth;
Try what my credit can in Venice do.   180
That shall be racked° even to the uttermost
To furnish thee to Belmont, to fair Portia.
Go presently° inquire, and so will I,
Where money is; and I no question make
To have it of my trust or for my sake.°   *Exeunt.* 183

---

160 **prest unto it** ready to aid you in it (from Latin *praesto*, at hand, ready)   161 **richly left** left rich   163 **virtues** powers and gifts (a more inclusive word than today)   165–66 **nothing undervalued/To** of no less value than   166 **Brutus' Portia** famed for her intellectual gifts, her resolution, and her wifely devotion (see *Julius Caesar*, II.i. 233–308)   171 **seat** estate   171 **Colchos' strond** the shore east of the Black Sea where Jason won the Golden Fleece   175 **a mind presages** me a presentiment that foretells me   175 **thrift** thriving, success   178 **commodity** merchandise   181 **racked** stretched to the point of torture (as on the rack)   183 **presently** instantly   185 **of my trust or for my sake** on my credit or on the basis of friendship

[Scene II. *Belmont. Portia's house.*]

Enter Portia with her waiting woman, Nerissa.

Portia. By my troth,° Nerissa, my little body is aweary
of this great world.

Nerissa. You would be, sweet madam, if your miseries
were in the same abundance as your good fortunes
5   are; and yet for aught I see, they are as sick that sur-
feit° with too much as they that starve with nothing.
It is no mean° happiness, therefore, to be seated in
the mean;° superfluity comes sooner by° white hairs,
but competency° lives longer.

10 *Portia.* Good sentences,° and well pronounced.

Nerissa. They would be better if well followed.

Portia. If to do were as easy to know what were good
to do, chapels had been° churches, and poor men's
cottages princes' palaces. It is a good divine that fol-
15 lows his own instructions; I can easier teach twenty
what were good to be done, than to be one of the
twenty to follow mine own teaching. The brain may
devise laws for the blood,° but a hot temper° leaps
o'er a cold decree;° such a hare is madness the youth
20 to skip o'er the meshes° of good counsel the cripple.
But this reasoning is not in the fashion° to choose me
a husband. O me, the word "choose"! I may neither
choose who I would nor refuse who I dislike, so is
the will of a living daughter curbed by the will° of

I ii.1 **troth** faith   5–6 **surfeit** are overfed, glutted   7, 8 **mean** (1)
slight (2) golden mean   8 **comes sooner by** acquires sooner   9 **com-
petency a** modest but comfortable fortune   10 **sentences** sententious
maxims   13 **had been** would have been   18 **blood** passion   18 **hot
temper** ardent temperament   19 **cold decree** decision made in cold
judgment   20 **meshes** nets for catching small creatures   21 **in the
fashion** of the sort   24 **will . . . will** wish . . . last will and testament

a dead father. Is it not hard, Nerissa, that I cannot   25
choose one, nor refuse none?°

Nerissa. Your father was ever virtuous, and holy men
at their death have good inspirations. Therefore the
lott'ry that he hath devised in these three chests of
gold, silver, and lead, whereof who chooses his mean-   30
ing chooses you, will no doubt never be chosen by
any rightly but one who you shall rightly love. But
what warmth is there in your affection towards any of
these princely suitors that are already come?

Portia. I pray thee overname them; and as thou namest   35
them I will describe them, and according to my description level at my affection.

Nerissa. First, there is the Neapolitan prince.

Portia. Ay, that's a colt indeed, for he doth nothing but
talk of his horse, and he makes it a great appropri-   40
ation to his own good parts° that he can shoe him
himself. I am much afeard my lady his mother
played false with a smith.

Nerissa. Then is there the County° Palatine.

Portia. He doth nothing but frown—as who should say,   45
"And° you will not have me, choose!" He hears
merry tales and smiles not; I fear he will prove the
weeping philosopher° when he grows old, being so
full of unmannerly sadness° in his youth. I had
rather be married to a death's-head with a bone in   50
his mouth than to either of these. God defend me
from these two!

Nerissa. How say you by the French lord, Monsieur Le
Bon?

Portia. God made him, and therefore let him pass for a   55
man. In truth, I know it is a sin to be a mocker, but

---

26 **refuse none** refuse any   40–41 **appropriation . . . parts** personal
accomplishment added to his talents   44 **County** Count   46 **And** if
47–48 **the weeping philosopher** i.e., another Heraclitus   49 **unmannerly sadness** unbecoming seriousness

he! Why, he hath a horse better than the Neapolitan's,
a better bad habit of frowning than the Count Palatine; he is every man in no man. If a throstle° sing,
60   he falls straight a-cap'ring; he will fence with his own
shadow. If I should° marry him, I should° marry
twenty husbands. If he would despise me, I would
forgive him; for if he love me to madness, I shall
never requite him.

65   *Nerissa.* What say you then to Falconbridge, the young
baron of England?

Portia. You know I say nothing to him, for he understands not me, nor I him. He hath neither Latin,
French, nor Italian; and you will come into the court
70   and swear that I have a poor pennyworth in the English. He is a proper° man's picture, but alas, who can
converse with a dumbshow? How oddly he is suited!
I think he bought his doublet° in Italy, his round
hose° in France, his bonnet in Germany, and his be-
75   havior everywhere.

Nerissa. What think you of the Scottish lord, his neighbor?

Portia. That he hath a neighborly charity in him, for he
borrowed a box of the ear of the Englishman and
80   swore he would pay him again when he was able. I
think the Frenchman° became his surety and sealed
under for another.

Nerissa. How like you the young German,° the Duke of
Saxony's nephew?

85   *Portia.* Very vilely in the morning when he is sober, and
most vilely in the afternoon when he is drunk. When
he is best he is a little worse than a man, and when he

59 throstle song thrush   61 should ... should were to ... would be
obliged to   71 proper handsome   73 doublet upper garment, cor-
responding to the modern coat   73-74 round hose lower garment,
combining the functions of breeches and stockings   76-81 Scottish
lord ... Frenchman (an allusion to the French promises of aid to the
Scots against the English, promises that were often broken)   83 German (Germans were proverbially heavy drinkers)

is worst he is little better than a beast.° And the worst
fall that ever fell, I hope I shall make shift° to go
without him.   90

Nerissa. If he should offer to choose, and choose the
right casket, you should refuse to perform your
father's will if you should refuse to accept him.

Portia. Therefore, for fear of the worst, I pray thee set
a deep glass of Rhenish wine on the contrary casket,   95
for if the devil be within and that temptation without,
I know he will choose it. I will do anything, Nerissa,
ere I will be married to a sponge.

Nerissa. You need not fear, lady, the having any of these
lords. They have acquainted me with their determi-   100
nations; which is indeed to return to their home, and
to trouble you with no more suit, unless you may be
won by some other sort° than your father's imposition,° depending on the caskets.

Portia. If I live to be as old as Sibylla,° I will die as   105
chaste as Diana unless I be obtained by the manner
of my father's will. I am glad this parcel of wooers
are so reasonable, for there is not one among them but
I dote on his very absence; and I pray God grant them
a fair departure.   110

Nerissa. Do you not remember, lady, in your father's
time, a Venetian, a scholar and a soldier, that came
hither in company of the Marquis of Montferrat?

Portia. Yes, yes, it was Bassanio!—as I think, so was he
called.   115

Nerissa. True, madam. He, of all the men that ever my
foolish eyes looked upon, was the best deserving a
fair lady.

87–88 best . . . beast (a pun, "beast" being pronounced almost like
"best." Such quibbles were not necessarily comic, but were considered clever and interesting)   89 make shift find a way   103 sort
manner   103–04 imposition command   105 Sibylla the Cumean
Sibyl (Apollo promised her as many years of life as were the grains
of sand she was holding in her hand)

Portia. I remember him well, and I remember him
120   worthy of thy praise.

Enter a Servingman.

How now? What news?

Servingman. The four strangers° seek for you, madam,
  to take their leave; and there is a forerunner come
  from a fifth, the Prince of Morocco, who brings word
125   the Prince his master will be here tonight.

Portia. If I could bid the fifth welcome with so good
  heart as I can bid the other four farewell, I should
  be glad of his approach. If he have the condition of a
  saint and the complexion of a devil, I had rather he
130   should shrive me than wive me. Come, Nerissa. Sirrah,° go before. Whiles we shut the gate upon one
  wooer, another knocks at the door.   *Exeunt.*

[Scene III. *Venice. A public place.*]

Enter Bassanio with Shylock the Jew.

Shylock. Three thousand ducats—well.

Bassanio. Ay, sir, for three months.

Shylock. For three months—well.

Bassanio. For the which, as I told you, Antonio shall be
5   bound.°

Shylock. Antonio shall become bound—well.

---

122 **four strangers** (apparently Shakespeare originally described four
suitors, then added two more, and forgot to change "four" to "six")
130–31 **Sirrah** (a regular form of address to a social inferior. Portia
speaks to the servant)   I.iii.5 **bound** under legal obligation as co-
signer of the bond

Bassanio. May° you stead° me? Will you pleasure me? Shall I know your answer?

Shylock. Three thousand ducats for three months, and Antonio bound.   10

Bassanio. Your answer to that.

Shylock. Antonio is a good man.°

Bassanio. Have you heard any imputation to the contrary?

Shylock. Ho no, no, no, no! My meaning in saying he is   15
a good man, is to have you understand me that he is
sufficient.° Yet his means are in supposition:° he hath
an argosy bound to Tripolis, another to the Indies; I
understand, moreover, upon the Rialto,° he hath a
third at Mexico, a fourth for England—and other   20
ventures he hath, squand'red abroad. But ships are
but boards, sailors but men; there be land rats and
water rats, water thieves and land thieves—I mean
pirates°—and then there is the peril of waters, winds,
and rocks. The man is, notwithstanding, sufficient.   25
Three thousand ducats—I think I may take his bond.

Bassanio. Be assured you may.

Shylock. I will be assured I may. And that I may be assured, I will bethink me. May I speak with Antonio?

Bassanio. If it please you to dine with us.   30

Shylock. Yes, to smell pork, to eat of the habitation
which your prophet the Nazarite° conjured the devil
into! I will buy with you, sell with you, talk with you,
walk with you, and so following; but I will not eat
with you, drink with you, nor pray with you. What   35
news on the Rialto? Who is he comes here?

7 **May** can   7 **stead** be of service to   12 **good man** good business
risk (Bassanio takes the word as referring to moral character)   17
sufficient adequate, responsible   17 **in supposition** doubtful   19
Rialto famous bridge in Venice, the center of commercial activity
24 **pirates** (pronounced "pi-rats," with quibble on "rats")   32 **the
Nazarite** Christ (the allusion is to the episode in Mark 5:1-13, Luke
8:26–33)

Enter Antonio.

Bassanio. This is Signior Antonio.

Shylock. [*Aside*] How like a fawning publican° he
      looks.
      I hate him for° he is a Christian;
40   But more, for that in low simplicity
      He lends out money gratis, and brings down
      The rate of usance° here with us in Venice.
      If I can catch him once upon the hip,°
      I will feed fat the ancient grudge I bear him.
45   He hates our sacred nation, and he rails,
      Even there where merchants most do congregate,
      On me, my bargains, and my well-won thrift,°
      Which he calls interest. Cursèd be my tribe
      If I forgive him.

Bassanio.   Shylock, do you hear?

50   **Shylock.** I am debating of my present store,°
      And by the near guess of my memory
      I cannot instantly raise up the gross°
      Of full three thousand ducats. What of that?
      Tubal, a wealthy Hebrew of my tribe,
55   Will furnish me. But soft,° how many months
      Do you desire? [*To Antonio*] Rest you fair, good
          signior!
      Your worship was the last man in our mouths.

Antonio. Shylock, albeit I neither lend nor borrow
      By taking nor by giving of excess,
60   Yet to supply the ripe wants of my friend,
      I'll break a custom. [*To Bassanio*] Is he yet pos-
          sessed°
      How much ye would?°

38 **publican** (sometimes glossed as a Roman tax-gatherer, as in Matthew 11:17 and 31:30 f., and sometimes as an Elizabethan innkeeper.
Perhaps Shylock uses it as an inexact but bitter term of reproach)
39 **for** because   42 **usance** interest   43 **upon the hip** at a disadvan-
tage (a term in wrestling)   47 **thrift** prosperity   50 **present store**
stock of ready money   52 **gross** whole amount   55 **soft** hold, stay
61 **possessed** apprised   62 **would** desire

Shylock.   Ay, ay, three thousand ducats.

Antonio. And for three months.

Shylock. I had forgot—three months, you told me so.
Well then, your bond. And let me see—but hear you: 65
Methoughts° you said you neither lend nor borrow
Upon advantage.°

Antonio.   I do never use it.

Shylock. When Jacob° grazed his uncle Laban's
     sheep—
This Jacob from our holy Abram was,
As his wise mother wrought in his behalf,   70
The third possessor; ay, he was the third—

Antonio. And what of him? Did he take interest?

Shylock. No, not take interest—not as you would say
Directly int'rest. Mark what Jacob did:
When Laban and himself were compremised°   75
That all the eanlings which were streaked and pied
Should fall as Jacob's hire, the ewes being rank
In end of autumn turnèd to the rams;
And when the work of generation was
Between these woolly breeders in the act,   80
The skillful shepherd pilled° me° certain wands,
And in the doing of the deed of kind°
He stuck them up before the fulsome ewes,
Who then conceiving, did in eaning° time
Fall parti-colored lambs, and those were Jacob's.   85
This was a way to thrive, and he was blest;
And thrift is blessing if men steal it not.

Antonio. This was a venture,° sir, that Jacob served for,
A thing not in his power to bring to pass,
But swayed and fashioned by the hand of heaven.   90
Was this inserted to make interest good?
Or is your gold and silver ewes and rams?

66 **Methoughts** it seemed to me   67 **advantage** interest   68 **Jacob**
(see Genesis 30:25–43; 31:1–13)   75 **were compremised** had reached
an agreement   81 **pilled** stripped   81 **me** (the ethical dative)   82
kind nature   84 **eaning** lambing   88 **venture** unpredictable enterprise

Shylock. I cannot tell; I make it breed as fast.
But note me, signior—

Antonio.   Mark you this, Bassanio,
95   The devil can cite Scripture for his purpose.
An evil soul producing holy witness
Is like a villain with a smiling cheek,
A goodly° apple rotten at the heart.
O what a goodly outside falsehood hath!

Shylock. Three thousand ducats—'tis a good round
100   sum.
Three months from twelve—then let me see, the
rate—

Antonio. Well, Shylock, shall we be beholding° to you?

Shylock. Signior Antonio, many a time and oft
In the Rialto you have rated° me
105   About my moneys and my usances.
Still° have I borne it with a patient shrug,
For suff'rance° is the badge of all our tribe.
You call me misbeliever, cutthroat dog,
And spet upon my Jewish gaberdine,°
110   And all for use of that which is mine own.
Well then, it now appears you need my help.
Go to, then.° You come to me and you say,
"Shylock, we would have moneys"—you say so,
You that did void your rheum° upon my beard
115   And foot me as you spurn a stranger cur
Over your threshold! Moneys is your suit.
What should I say to you? Should I not say,
"Hath a dog money? Is it possible
A cur can lend three thousand ducats?" Or
120   Shall I bend low, and in a bondman's key,
With bated breath, and whisp'ring humbleness,
Say this:

98 **goodly** fine-appearing   102 **beholding** beholden, obligated   104 **rated** berated, reviled   106 **Still** always   107 **suff'rance** long-suffering   109 **gaberdine** the distinctive gown or mantle of the Jews   112 **Go to, then** (an exclamation suggesting annoyance)   114 **rheum** spittle

"Fair sir, you spet on me on Wednesday last,
You spurned me such a day, another time
You called me dog; and for these courtesies
I'll lend you thus much moneys"?   *125*

Antonio. I am as like to call thee so again,
To spet on thee again, to spurn thee too.
If thou wilt lend this money, lend it not
As to thy friends—for when did friendship take   *130*
A breed for barren metal° of his friend?—
But lend it rather to thine enemy,
Who if he break,° thou mayst with better face
Exact the penalty.

Shylock.   Why look you, how you storm!
I would be friends with you, and have your love,   *135*
Forget the shames that you have stained me with,
Supply your present wants, and take no doit°
Of usance for my moneys; and you'll not hear me.
This is kind° I offer.

Bassanio. This were kindness.

Shylock.   This kindness will I show: *140*
Go with me to a notary; seal me there
Your single° bond, and, in a merry sport,
If you repay me not on such a day,
In such a place, such sum or sums as are
Expressed in the condition, let the forfeit   *145*
Be nominated for an equal pound
Of your fair flesh, to be cut off and taken
In what part of your body pleaseth me.

Antonio. Content, in faith. I'll seal to such a bond,
And say there is much kindness° in the Jew.   *150*

Bassanio. You shall not seal to such a bond for me!
I'll rather dwell in my necessity.

131 breed for barren metal interest (Aristotelian doctrine held that
money, unlike living things, cannot reproduce)   133 break become
insolvent   137 doit tiny Dutch coin, valued at one-eighth of an
English penny   139 kind kind and natural (in contrast to usurious
dealings)   142 single without further security   150 kindness natural
friendliness

Antonio. Why fear not, man; I will not forfeit it.
Within these two months—that's a month before
155 This bond expires—I do expect return
Of thrice three times the value of this bond.

Shylock. O father Abram, what these Christians are,
Whose own hard dealings teaches them suspect
The thoughts of others! Pray you tell me this:
160 If he should break his day,° what should I gain
By the exaction of the forfeiture?
A pound of man's flesh taken from a man
Is not so estimable, profitable neither,
As flesh of muttons, beefs, or goats. I say
165 To buy his favor I extend this friendship.
If he will take it, so; if not, adieu.°
And for my love I pray you wrong me not.°

Antonio. Yes, Shylock, I will seal unto this bond.

Shylock. Then meet me forthwith at the notary's;
170 Give him direction for this merry bond,
And I will go and purse the ducats straight,
See to my house, left in the fearful° guard
Of an unthrifty knave,° and presently°
I'll be with you.   *Exit.*

Antonio.   Hie thee, gentle Jew.°
175 The Hebrew will turn Christian; he grows kind.

Bassanio. I like not fair terms and a villain's mind.

Antonio. Come on. In this there can be no dismay;
My ships come home a month before the day.
                                        Exeunt.

---

160 **break his day** break his promise to pay on the due date   166
adieu (probably the word has the original meaning, "I commend
you to God")   167 **And ... wrong me not** i.e., and for the friendship I have shown you, please don't misjudge me in the future
172 **fearful** hazardous   173 **unthrifty knave** careless youngster   173
presently instantly   174 **gentle Jew** courteous Jew (with a pun on
"gentile")

[ACT II

Scene I. *Belmont. Portia's house.*]

[Flourish of cornets.] Enter [the Prince of]
Morocco, a tawny Moor all in white, and three or
four Followers accordingly, with Portia, Nerissa,
and their Train.

Morocco. Mislike me not for my complexion,
The shadowed° livery° of the burnished sun,
To whom I am a neighbor and near bred.
Bring me the fairest creature northward born,
Where Phoebus'° fire scarce thaws the icicles,   5
And let us make incision° for your love
To prove whose blood is reddest, his or mine.
I tell thee, lady, this aspect° of mine
Hath feared the valiant.° By my love I swear,
The best-regarded virgins of our clime   10
Have loved it too. I would not change this hue,
Except to steal your thoughts, my gentle queen.

Portia. In terms of choice° I am not solely led
By nice° direction of a maiden's eyes.
Besides, the lott'ry of my destiny   15

II.i.2 **shadowed** dark   2 **livery** uniform for a king's or nobleman's
retainers   5 **Phoebus'** the sun-god's   6 **make incision** cut our flesh
8 **aspect** (pronounced "a-spèct")   9 **feared the valiant** caused the
valiant to fear   13 **In terms of choice** with respect to my choice
14 **nice** fastidious

Bars me the right of voluntary choosing.
But if my father had not scanted° me,
And hedged me by his wit° to yield myself
His wife who wins me by that means I told you,
20   Yourself, renownèd Prince, then stood as fair
As any comer I have looked on yet
For my affection.

Morocco.   Even for that I thank you.
Therefore I pray you lead me to the caskets
To try my fortune. By this scimitar,
25   That slew the Sophy,° and a Persian prince
That won three fields of Sultan Solyman,
I would o'erstare° the sternest eyes that look,
Outbrave the heart most daring on the earth,
Pluck the young sucking cubs from the she-bear,
30   Yea, mock the lion when 'a° roars for prey,
To win thee, lady. But alas the while,
If Hercules and Lichas° play at dice
Which is the better man, the greater throw
May turn by fortune from the weaker hand.
35   So is Alcides° beaten by his page,
And so may I, blind Fortune leading me,
Miss that which one unworthier may attain,
And die with grieving.

Portia.   You must take your chance,
And either not attempt to choose at all,
40   Or swear before you choose, if you choose wrong
Never to speak to lady afterward
In way of marriage. Therefore be advised.°

Morocco. Nor will not.° Come, bring me unto my
chance.

Portia. First, forward to the temple; after dinner
Your hazard shall be made.

---

17 **scanted** limited   18 **hedged me by his wit** fenced me in by his
clever intellect   25 **Sophy** Shah of Persia   27 **o'erstare** outstare
30 **'a** he   32 **Lichas** Hercules' page   35 **Alcides** Hercules   42 **be
advised** consider well   43 **Nor will not** nor will I (ever woo another
for my wife)

Morocco.   Good fortune then,   45
To make me blest or cursèd'st among men!
                              [*Flourish of cornets.*] *Exeunt.*

[Scene II. *Venice. A street.*]

Enter [*Launcelot Gobbo,*] *the Clown, alone.*

Launcelot. Certainly my conscience will serve me to
run from this Jew my master. The fiend is at
mine elbow and tempts me, saying to me, "Gobbo,
Launcelot Gobbo, good Launcelot," or "good
Gobbo," or "good Launcelot Gobbo—use your   5
legs, take the start, run away." My conscience says,
"No. Take heed, honest Launcelot; take heed,
honest Gobbo," or as aforesaid, "honest Launcelot
Gobbo, do not run; scorn running with thy heels."°
Well, the most courageous fiend bids me pack.   10
"Fia!"° says the fiend; "away!" says the fiend. "For
the heavens,° rouse up a brave mind," says the
fiend, "and run." Well, my conscience hanging about
the neck of my heart says very wisely to me, "My
honest friend Launcelot, being an honest man's   15
son"—or rather an honest woman's son, for indeed
my father did something smack, something grow
to, he had a kind of taste°—Well, my conscience
says, "Launcelot, budge not." "Budge," says the
fiend. "Budge not," says my conscience. "Con-   20
science," say I, "you counsel well." "Fiend," say I,
"you counsel well." To be ruled by my conscience,

II.ii. 9 **scorn running with thy heels** (1) scorn to run away with your
feet (2) scorn utterly to run   11 **Fia!** (from Italian *via*, away)   11–12
For the heavens by heaven, or for heaven's sake (in either case a
grotesque thing for the fiend to say)   17–18 **did something smack**
··· **had a kind of taste** (both phrases indicate a tendency to vice)

I should stay with the Jew my master who (God
bless the mark!)° is a kind of devil; and to run away
25 from the Jew, I should be ruled by the fiend who,
saving your reverence, is the devil himself. Certainly
the Jew is the very devil incarnation;° and in my
conscience, my conscience is but a kind of hard conscience to offer to counsel me to stay with the Jew.
30 The fiend gives the more friendly counsel. I will run,
fiend; my heels are at your commandment, I will
run.

Enter Old Gobbo with a basket.

Gobbo. Master young man, you, I pray you, which is
the way to Master Jew's?

35 *Launcelot.* [*Aside*] O heavens, this is my true-begotten
father who, being more than sand-blind,° high-
gravel-blind,° knows me not. I will try confusions
with him.

Gobbo. Master young gentleman, I pray you which is
40 the way to Master Jew's?

Launcelot. Turn up on your right hand at the next
turning, but at the next turning of all, on your left;
marry,° at the very next turning turn of no hand,
but turn down indirectly to the Jew's house.

45 *Gobbo.* Be God's sonties,° 'twill be a hard way to hit!
Can you tell me whether one Launcelot that dwells
with him, dwell with him or no?

Launcelot. Talk you of young Master Launcelot?
[*Aside*] Mark me now! Now will I raise the
50 waters.°—Talk you of young Master Launcelot?

23–24 **God bless the mark!** (used, like "saving your reverence" in
line 26, to avert a bad omen)   27 **Incarnation** (blunder for "in-
carnate")   36 **sand-blind** dull of sight   36–37 **high-gravel-blind**
(Launcelot's comic superlative for "sand-blind")   43 **marry** (a
mild interjection, originally an oath, by the Virgin Mary)   45 **Be
God's sonties** by God's little saints   49–50 **raise the waters** rouse a
storm of emotion (a nautical metaphor?)

Gobbo. No master,° sir, but a poor man's son. His
father, though I say't, is an honest exceeding poor
man and, God be thanked, well to live.°

Launcelot. Well, let his father be what 'a will, we talk
of young Master Launcelot.   55

Gobbo. Your worship's friend,° and Launcelot, sir.

Launcelot. But I pray you, ergo° old man, ergo I beseech you, talk you of young Master Launcelot?

Gobbo. Of Launcelot, an't° please your mastership.

Launcelot. Ergo, Master Launcelot. Talk not of Master   60
Launcelot, father, for the young gentleman, according to Fates and Destinies and such odd sayings, the
Sisters Three and such branches of learning, is indeed deceased, or as you would say in plain terms,
gone to heaven.   65

Gobbo. Marry, God forbid! The boy was the very staff
of my age, my very prop.

Launcelot. [*Aside*] Do I look like a cudgel or a hovel-
post, a staff, or a prop?° Do you know me, father?°

Gobbo. Alack the day, I know you not, young gentle-   70
man, but I pray you tell me, is my boy—God rest
his soul—alive or dead?

Launcelot. Do you not know me, father?°

Gobbo. Alack, sir, I am sand-blind! I know you not.

Launcelot. Nay, indeed if you had your eyes you might   75
fail of the knowing me. It is a wise father that knows
his own child. Well, old man, I will tell you news of
your son. [*Kneels, with his back to his father.*] Give
me your blessing. Truth will come to light; murder

51 **No master** (as a servant, Launcelot has no claim to the title of
master)   52–53 **exceeding . . . to live** poverty-stricken and well-to-do
56 **Your worship's friend** (he politely insists on his son's humble
status)   57 **ergo** therefore   59 **an't** if it   68–69 **Do I . . . a prop?**
(spoken directly to the audience)   69, 73 **father** (a term of courtesy
often used by the young to the old, without implying blood relationship)

80 cannot be hid long—a man's son may, but in the
end truth will out.

Gobbo. Pray you, sir, stand up. I am sure you are not
Launcelot, my boy.

Launcelot. Pray you let's have no more fooling about
85 it, but give me your blessing. I am Launcelot—your
boy that was, your son that is, your child that
shall be.

Gobbo. I cannot think you are my son.

Launcelot. I know not what I shall think of that; but
90 I am Launcelot, the Jew's man, and I am sure
Margery your wife is my mother.

Gobbo. Her name is Margery indeed! I'll be sworn, if
thou be Launcelot thou art mine own flesh and
blood. Lord worshipped might he be, what a beard°
95 hast thou got! Thou hast got more hair on thy chin
than Dobbin my fill-horse° has on his tail.

Launcelot. [*Rises*] It should seem then that Dobbin's
tail grows backward. I am sure he had more hair of
his tail than I have of my face when I last saw him.

100 *Gobbo.* Lord, how art thou changed! How dost thou
and thy master agree? I have brought him a present.
How 'gree you now?

Launcelot. Well, well; but for mine own part, as I have
set up my rest° to run away, so I will not rest till I
105 have run some ground. My master's a very Jew. Give
him a present? Give him a halter!° I am famished
in his service; you may tell° every finger I have with
my ribs. Father, I am glad you are come. Give me
your present to one Master Bassanio, who indeed
110 gives rare new liveries. If I serve not him I will run

94 beard (the sand-blind father places his hand on his son's head,
and mistakes Launcelot's fashionable long hair for a huge beard)
96 fill-horse cart horse   104 set up my rest wagered all (with word
play on "rest" and "run")   106 halter hangman's noose   107 tell
count

as far as God has any ground. O rare fortune, here
comes the man. To him, father, for I am a Jew if
I serve the Jew any longer.

*Enter Bassanio, with [Leonardo and] a Follower
or two.*

Bassanio. You may do so, but let it be so hasted that
supper be ready at the farthest by five of the clock.   *115*
See these letters delivered, put the liveries to making,
and desire Gratiano to come anon° to my lodging.
                              [*Exit one of his men.*]

Launcelot. To him, father!

Gobbo. God bless your worship!

Bassanio. Gramercy.° Wouldst thou aught with me?   *120*

Gobbo. Here's my son, sir, a poor boy—

Launcelot. Not a poor boy, sir, but the rich Jew's man,
that would, sir, as my father shall specify—

Gobbo. He hath a great infection,° sir, as one would
say, to serve—   *125*

Launcelot. Indeed, the short and the long is, I serve
the Jew, and have a desire, as my father shall
specify—

Gobbo. His master and he, saving your worship's reverence, are scarce cater-cousins.°   *130*

Launcelot. To be brief, the very truth is that the Jew,
having done me wrong, doth cause me, as my father,
being I hope an old man, shall frutify° unto you—

Gobbo. I have here a dish of doves that I would bestow
upon your worship, and my suit is—   *135*

---

117 **anon** straightway   120 **Gramercy** many thanks (French *grand
merci*)   124 **infection** (Gobbo's mistake for "affection," i.e., liking)
130 **cater-cousins** great friends   133 **frutify** (for "fructify," a blunder for a word like "signify")

Launcelot. In very brief, the suit is impertinent° to myself, as your worship shall know by this honest old
man, and though I say it, though old man, yet poor
man, my father.

140 *Bassanio.* One speak for both. What would you?

Launcelot. Serve you, sir.

Gobbo. That is the very defect° of the matter, sir.

Bassanio. I know thee well; thou hast obtained thy suit.
Shylock thy master spoke with me this day,
145 And hath preferred° thee, if it be preferment
To leave a rich Jew's service to become
The follower of so poor a gentleman.

Launcelot. The old proverb° is very well parted between my master Shylock and you, sir. You have
150 the grace of God, sir, and he hath enough.

Bassanio. Thou speak'st it well. Go, father, with thy
son;
Take leave of thy old master and inquire
My lodging out. [*To a Servant*] Give him a livery
More guarded° than his fellows'. See it done.

155 *Launcelot.* Father, in. I cannot get a service; no! I have
ne'er a tongue in my head! Well! [*Studies his palm.*]
If any man in Italy have a fairer table° which doth
offer to swear upon a book—I shall have good fortune! Go to, here's a simple line of life. Here's a
160 small trifle of wives. Alas, fifteen wives is nothing;
eleven widows and nine maids is a simple coming-in
for one man. And then to scape drowning thrice,
and to be in peril of my life with the edge of a feather-
bed! Here are simple scapes.° Well, if Fortune be a
165 woman, she's a good wench for this gear.° Father,

---

136 **impertinent** (for "pertinent")   142 **defect** (for "effect")   145
preferred recommended for a higher position   148 **proverb** (such as,
"He that hath the grace of God hath enough")   154 **guarded** orna-
mented   157 **table** palm   164 **scapes** escapes   165 **gear** business,
i.e., the good fortune that he pretends to read in his palm

come. I'll take my leave of the Jew in the twinkling.
       Exit Clown [Launcelot, with Old Gobbo].

Bassanio. I pray thee, good Leonardo, think on this:
  These things being bought and orderly bestowed,
  Return in haste, for I do feast tonight
  My best-esteemed acquaintance. Hie thee, go.   *170*

Leonardo. My best endeavors shall be done herein.

             Enter Gratiano.

Gratiano. Where's your master?

Leonardo.   Yonder, sir, he walks.
                        Exit Leonardo.

Gratiano. Signior Bassanio!

Bassanio. Gratiano!

Gratiano. I have suit to you.

Bassanio.   You have obtained it!   *175*

Gratiano. You must not deny me. I must go with you
  to Belmont.

Bassanio. Why then you must. But hear thee, Gratiano:
  Thou art too wild, too rude, and bold of voice—
  Parts that become thee happily enough
  And in such eyes as ours appear not faults;   *180*
  But where thou art not known—why, there they
    show
  Something too liberal.° Pray thee take pain
  To allay with some cold drops of modesty
  Thy skipping spirit, lest through thy wild behavior
  I be misconst'red° in the place I go to,   *185*
  And lose my hopes.

Gratiano.   Signior Bassanio, hear me:
  If I do not put on a sober habit,°
  Talk with respect, and swear but now and then,

---

182 liberal free (a kind word to describe Gratiano!) 185 misconst'red misconstrued 187 habit (1) bearing (2) garment

Wear prayer books in my pocket, look demurely—
190   Nay more, while grace is saying hood mine eyes
Thus with my hat, and sigh and say Amen,
Use all the observance of civility°
Like one well studied in a sad ostent°
To please his grandam, never trust me more.

195 *Bassanio.* Well, we shall see your bearing.

Gratiano. Nay, but I bar tonight. You shall not gauge
     me
By what we do tonight.

Bassanio.   No, that were pity.
I would entreat you rather to put on
Your boldest suit of mirth, for we have friends
200   That purpose merriment. But fare you well;
I have some business.

Gratiano. And I must to Lorenzo and the rest,
But we will visit you at supper time.   *Exeunt.*

[Scene III. *Venice. Shylock's house.*]

Enter Jessica and [Launcelot] the Clown.

Jessica. I am sorry thou wilt leave my father so;
Our house is hell, and thou a merry devil
Didst rob it of some taste of tediousness.
But fare thee well; there is a ducat for thee.
5   And, Launcelot, soon at supper shalt thou see
Lorenzo, who is thy new master's guest.
Give him this letter; do it secretly.
And so farewell. I would not have my father
See me in talk with thee.

192 **civility** civilized behavior   193 **sad ostent** sober and earnest
appearance

Launcelot. Adieu!° Tears exhibit° my tongue. Most   10
  beautiful pagan, most sweet Jew, if a Christian do
  not play the knave and get thee, I am much deceived.° But adieu! These foolish drops do something drown my manly spirit. Adieu!

Jessica. Farewell, good Launcelot.   [*Exit Launcelot.*]   15
  Alack, what heinous sin is it in me
  To be ashamed to be my father's child!
  But though I am a daughter to his blood,
  I am not to his manners. O Lorenzo,
  If thou keep promise, I shall end this strife,   20
  Become a Christian and thy loving wife!   *Exit.*

[Scene IV. *Venice. A street.*]

Enter Gratiano, Lorenzo, Salerio, and Solanio.

Lorenzo. Nay, we will slink away in supper time,
  Disguise us at my lodging, and return
  All in an hour.

Gratiano. We have not made good preparation.

Salerio. We have not spoke us yet of torchbearers.°   5

Solanio. 'Tis vile, unless it may be quaintly ordered,°
  And better in my mind not undertook.

Lorenzo. 'Tis now but four of clock. We have two
  hours
  To furnish us.

II.iii.10 **Adieu** (perhaps not merely "good-bye," but "I commend you
to God")   10 **exhibit** (for "inhibit")   11–13 **if a . . . deceived** (perhaps Launcelot is giving a hint of what happens in II.v, but perhaps
"do" should be emended to "did," and "get" should be understood
in the sense of "beget")   II.iv.5 **spoke us yet of torchbearers** talked
about getting torchbearers (who were regularly used in this sort of
street festivity)   6 **quaintly ordered** artfully arranged

Enter Launcelot [with a letter].

Friend Launcelot, what's the news?

10 *Launcelot.* And it shall please you to break up° this,
it shall seem to signify.

Lorenzo. I know the hand. In faith, 'tis a fair hand,
And whiter than the paper it° writ on
Is the fair hand that writ.

Gratiano.   Love-news, in faith!

15 *Launcelot.* By your leave, sir.

Lorenzo. Whither goest thou?

Launcelot. Marry, sir, to bid° my old master the Jew
to sup tonight with my new master the Christian.

Lorenzo. Hold here, take this. [*Gives money.*] Tell
gentle° Jessica
20 I will not fail her. Speak it privately.
                              Exit Clown [Launcelot].
Go, gentlemen;
Will you prepare you for this masque tonight?
I am provided of a torchbearer.

Salerio. Ay marry, I'll be gone about it straight.

Solanio. And so will I.

25 *Lorenzo.*   Meet me and Gratiano
At Gratiano's lodging some hour hence.

Salerio. 'Tis good we do so.   *Exit [with Solanio].*

Gratiano. Was not that letter from fair Jessica?

Lorenzo. I must needs tell thee all. She hath directed
30 How I shall take her from her father's house,
What gold and jewels she is furnished with,
What page's suit she hath in readiness.
If e'er the Jew her father come to heaven,

10 **break up** open   13 **it** i.e., the hand   17 **bid** ask   19, 34 **gentle**
charming and possessed of all attributes of a lady (with a pun on
"gentile," as elsewhere)

It will be for his gentle daughter's sake;
And never dare misfortune cross her foot,°   35
Unless she do it under this excuse,
That she is issue to a faithless° Jew.
Come, go with me; peruse this as thou goest.
Fair Jessica shall be my torchbearer.°
                                    Exit [with Gratiano].

[Scene V. *Venice. Before Shylock's house.*]

*Enter [Shylock the] Jew and [Launcelot,] his man
that was the Clown.*

Shylock. Well, thou shalt see, thy eyes shall be thy
     judge,
The difference of old Shylock and Bassanio.—
What,° Jessica!—Thou shalt not gormandize
As thou hast done with me.—What, Jessica!—
And sleep, and snore, and rend apparel out.—   5
Why, Jessica, I say!

Launcelot.   Why, Jessica!

Shylock. Who bids thee call? I do not bid thee call.

Launcelot. Your worship was wont to tell me I could
     do nothing without bidding.

                    Enter Jessica.

Jessica. Call you? What is your will?   10

Shylock. I am bid forth to supper, Jessica.
There are my keys. But wherefore should I go?
I am not bid for love—they flatter me.
But yet I'll go in hate, to feed upon
The prodigal Christian. Jessica my girl,   15

35 **cross her foot** cross her path   37 **faithless** lacking the Christian
faith   39 **torchbearer** i.e., disguised as a page   **II.v.3 What** (exclamation of impatience, like "Why" in line 6)

Look to my house. I am right loath to go.
There is some ill a-brewing towards my rest,
For I did dream of moneybags tonight.°

Launcelot. I beseech you, sir, go. My young master
20   doth expect your reproach.°

Shylock. So do I his.

Launcelot. And they have conspired together. I will
not say you shall see a masque, but if you do, then
it was not for nothing that my nose fell a-bleeding
23   on Black Monday° last at six o'clock i' th' morning,
falling out that year on Ash Wednesday was four
year in th' afternoon.°

Shylock. What, are there masques? Hear you me,
Jessica:
Lock up my doors; and when you hear the drum
30   And the vile squealing of the wry-necked fife,°
Clamber not you up to the casements then,
Nor thrust your head into the public street
To gaze on Christian fools with varnished faces;°
But stop my house's ears—I mean my casements;
33   Let not the sound of shallow fopp'ry enter
My sober house. By Jacob's staff I swear
I have no mind of feasting forth tonight;
But I will go. Go you before me, sirrah.
Say I will come.

Launcelot.   I will go before, sir.
40   Mistress, look out at window for all this:
There will come a Christian by
Will be worth a Jewess' eye.   [*Exit.*]

18 **tonight** last night (the premonition is serious for Shylock, comic
for the audience)   20 **reproach** (Launcelot's word for "approach")
25 **Black Monday** Easter Monday   26–27 **falling . . . afternoon**
(apparently Launcelot means "four years ago on Ash Wednesday,"
but he may be intentionally talking nonsense)   30 **wry-necked fife**
fife-player with neck twisted to one side (the mouthpiece of the
Elizabethan fife was set at an angle, and these words are therefore
sometimes taken to mean the instrument; but Shylock would be
less scornful of the instrument than of the gay fool with his neck
at a crazy angle)   33 **varnished faces** painted masks (Shylock no
doubt puns on "varnished" in the sense of "insincere")

Shylock. What says that fool of Hagar's offspring,° ha?

Jessica. His words were "Farewell, mistress"—nothing
else.

Shylock. The patch° is kind enough, but a huge feeder,   45
Snail-slow in profit,° and he sleeps by day
More than the wildcat. Drones hive not with me;
Therefore I part with him, and part with him
To one that I would have him help to waste
His borrowed purse. Well, Jessica, go in;   50
Perhaps I will return immediately.
Do as I bid you, shut doors after you.
Fast bind, fast find,
A proverb never stale in thrifty mind.   *Exit.*

Jessica. Farewell; and if my fortune be not crost,   55
I have a father, you a daughter, lost.   *Exit.*

[Scene VI. *Venice. Before Shylock's house.*]

Enter the Masquers, Gratiano and Salerio.

Gratiano. This is the penthouse° under which Lorenzo
Desired us to make stand.

Salerio.   His hour is almost past.

Gratiano. And it is marvel he outdwells his hour,
For lovers ever run before the clock.

Salerio. O ten times faster Venus' pigeons° fly   5
To seal love's bonds new-made, than they are wont
To keep obligèd faith° unforfeited!

---

43 **Hagar's offspring** Ishmael, son of Abraham by the servant Hagar
(mother and son were cast out by Abraham after Isaac's birth)
45 **patch** fool   46 **in profit** in any profitable activity   II.vi.1 **pent-
house** shelter formed by a projecting roof   5 **Venus' pigeons** (they
drew her chariot)   7 **obligèd faith** faith pledged (in marriage)

Gratiano. That ever holds. Who riseth from a feast
    With that keen appetite that he sits down?
10 Where is the horse that doth untread again
    His tedious measures° with the unbated fire
    That he did pace them first? All things that are
    Are with more spirit chasèd than enjoyed.
    How like a younger° or a prodigal
15 The scarfèd° bark puts from her native bay,
    Hugged and embracèd by the strumpet wind!
    How like the prodigal doth she return,
    With over-weathered° ribs and ragged sails,
    Lean, rent, and beggared by the strumpet wind!

Enter Lorenzo.

20 *Salerio.* Here comes Lorenzo: more of this hereafter.

Lorenzo. Sweet friends, your patience for my long
    abode.°
    Not I but my affairs have made you wait.
    When you shall please to play the thieves for wives,
    I'll watch as long for you then. Approach;
25 Here dwells my father Jew. Ho, who's within?

[Enter] Jessica above [in boy's clothes].

Jessica. Who are you? Tell me for more certainty,
    Albeit I'll swear that I do know your tongue.

Lorenzo. Lorenzo, and thy love.

Jessica. Lorenzo certain, and my love indeed,
30 For who love I so much? And now who knows
    But you, Lorenzo, whether I am yours?

Lorenzo. Heaven and thy thoughts are witness that
    thou art.

Jessica. Here, catch this casket; it is worth the pains.
    I am glad 'tis night, you° do not look on me,

---

11 **measures** paces 14 **younger** younger son 15 **scarfèd** decorated
with scarfs (i.e., flags and streamers) 18 **over-weathered** long exposed to stormy weather 21 **abode** delay 34 **'tis night, you** (an
ellipsis, "and" being understood

For I am much ashamed of my exchange.°   *35*
But love is blind, and lovers cannot see
The pretty follies that themselves commit;
For if they could, Cupid himself would blush
To see me thus transformèd to a boy.

Lorenzo. Descend, for you must be my torchbearer.   *40*

Jessica. What, must I hold a candle to my shames?
They in themselves, good sooth, are too too light.°
Why, 'tis an office of discovery,° love,
And I should be obscured.

Lorenzo.   So are you, sweet,
Even in the lovely garnish° of a boy.   *45*
But come at once;
For the close° night doth play the runaway,
And we are stayed for at Bassanio's feast.

Jessica. I will make fast the doors and gild myself
With some moe° ducats, and be with you straight.   *50*
                              [*Exit above.*]

Gratiano. Now by my hood, a gentle° and no Jew!

Lorenzo. Beshrow° me but I love her heartily!
For she is wise, if I can judge of her,
And fair she is, if that mine eyes be true,
And true she is, as she hath proved herself;   *55*
And therefore, like herself, wise, fair, and true,
Shall she be placèd in my constant soul.

                    Enter Jessica [*below*].

What, art thou come? On, gentlemen, away!
Our masquing mates by this time for us stay.
                    Exit [*with Jessica and Salerio*].

                    Enter Antonio.

Antonio. Who's there?   *60*

35 exchange i.e., of clothes   42 light immodest (with a pun)   43
office of discovery task in which my disguise will be revealed
45 garnish pleasing attire   47 close secret   50 moe more   51 gentle
refined lady (with the usual pun on "gentile")   52 Beshrow (a light
word for "curse")

Gratiano. Signior Antonio?

Antonio. Fie, fie, Gratiano, where are all the rest?
'Tis nine o'clock, our friends all stay for you.
No masque tonight. The wind is come about;
65 Bassanio presently° will go aboard.
I have sent twenty out to seek for you.

Gratiano. I am glad on't. I desire no more delight
Than to be under sail and gone tonight.   *Exeunt.*

[Scene VII. *Belmont. Portia's house.*]

[*Flourish of cornets.*] *Enter Portia with Morocco
and both their Trains.*

Portia. Go, draw aside the curtains and discover°
The several caskets to this noble Prince.
Now make your choice.

Morocco. This first, of gold, who this inscription bears,
"Who chooseth me shall gain what many men
5   desire."
The second, silver, which this promise carries,
"Who chooseth me shall get as much as he deserves."
This third, dull lead, with warning all as blunt,°
"Who chooseth me must give and hazard all he
hath."
10 How shall I know if I do choose the right?

Portia. The one of them contains my picture, Prince.
If you choose that, then I am yours withal.

Morocco. Some god direct my judgment! Let me see—

65 **presently** at this present moment II.vii.1 **discover** reveal 8 **as
blunt** as blunt as the lead is dull (with quibbles on "blunt" in the
senses of "abrupt in speech and manner" and of "not sharp," and
on "dull" in the senses of "not sharp" and "not shining")

I will survey th' inscriptions back again.
What says this leaden casket?   15
"Who chooseth me must give and hazard all he
    hath."
Must give—for what? For lead! Hazard for lead?
This casket threatens; men that hazard all
Do it in hope of fair advantages.
A golden mind stoops not to shows of dross;   20
I'll then nor give nor hazard aught for lead.
What says the silver with her virgin hue?
"Who chooseth me shall get as much as he deserves."
As much as he deserves? Pause there, Morocco,
And weigh thy value with an even hand: 25
If thou be'st rated by thy estimation,°
Thou dost deserve enough, and yet enough
May not extend so far as to the lady;
And yet to be afeard of my deserving
Were but a weak disabling° of myself.   30
As much as I deserve? Why that's the lady!
I do in birth deserve her, and in fortunes,
In graces, and in qualities of breeding;
But more than these, in love I do deserve.
What if I strayed no farther, but chose here?   35
Let's see once more this saying graved in gold:
"Who chooseth me shall gain what many men
    desire."
Why that's the lady! All the world desires her;
From the four corners of the earth they come
To kiss this shrine, this mortal breathing saint.   40
The Hyrcanian deserts° and the vasty wilds
Of wide Arabia are as throughfares now
For princes to come view fair Portia.
The watery kingdom, whose ambitious head
Spets in the face of heaven, is no bar   45
To stop the foreign spirits, but they come
As o'er a brook to see fair Portia.
One of these three contains her heavenly picture.
Is't like that lead contains her? 'Twere damnation

26 estimation reputation   30 disabling undervaluing   41 Hyrcanian
deserts Persian deserts (famous for savage beasts)

50   To think so base a thought; it were too gross°
     To rib her cerecloth° in the obscure° grave.
     Or shall I think in silver she's immured,
     Being ten times undervalued to tried gold?
     O sinful thought! Never so rich a gem
55   Was set in worse than gold. They have in England
     A coin that bears the figure of an angel
     Stampèd in gold—but that's insculped° upon;
     But here an angel° in a golden bed
     Lies all within. Deliver me the key.
60   Here do I choose, and thrive I as I may!

Portia. There, take it, Prince; and if my form lie there,
     Then I am yours.   [*He opens the golden casket.*]

Morocco.   O hell! What have we here?
     A carrion Death,° within whose empty eye
     There is a written scroll! I'll read the writing.
65   "All that glisters is not gold;°
        Often have you heard that told.
        Many a man his life hath sold
        But my outside to behold;
        Gilded tombs do worms infold.
70   Had you been as wise as bold,
        Young in limbs, in judgment old,
        Your answer had not been inscrolled.°
        Fare you well, your suit is cold."
     Cold indeed, and labor lost.
75   Then farewell heat, and welcome frost!
     Portia, adieu. I have too grieved a heart
     To take a tedious leave. Thus losers part.
                Exit [*with his Train. Flourish of cornets*].

Portia. A gentle° riddance. Draw the curtains, go.
     Let all of his complexion° choose me so.   *Exeunt.*

---

50 **it were too gross** lead would be too coarse (bodies of wealthy
persons were often encased in lead)   51 **cerecloth** waxed em-
balming cloth   51 **obscure** (accent on first syllable)   57 **insculped**
sculptured   58 **angel** i.e., Portia's picture   63 **Death** death's head
65 **All . . . gold** (proverbial)   72 **inscrolled** written on the scroll
78 **gentle** well-bred   79 **complexion** temperament (not merely col-
oring)

[Scene VIII. *Venice. A street.*]

Enter Salerio and Solanio.

Salerio. Why, man, I saw Bassanio under sail;
With him is Gratiano gone along,
And in their ship I am sure Lorenzo is not.

Solanio. The villain° Jew with outcries raised the Duke,
Who went with him to search Bassanio's ship.   5

Salerio. He came too late, the ship was under sail.
But there the Duke was given to understand
That in a gondola were seen together
Lorenzo and his amorous Jessica.
Besides, Antonio certified the Duke   10
They were not with Bassanio in his ship.

Solanio. I never heard a passion° so confused,
So strange, outrageous, and so variable
As the dog Jew did utter in the streets:
"My daughter! O my ducats! O my daughter!   15
Fled with a Christian! O my Christian ducats!
Justice! The law! My ducats and my daughter!
A sealèd bag, two sealèd bags of ducats,
Of double ducats, stol'n from me by my daughter!
And jewels—two stones, two rich and precious
    stones,
Stol'n by my daughter! Justice! Find the girl!   20
She hath the stones upon her, and the ducats!"

Salerio. Why, all the boys in Venice follow him,
Crying his stones, his daughter, and his ducats.

Solanio. Let good Antonio look he keep his day,°   25
Or he shall pay for this.

II.viii.4 **villain** low-bred fellow (not scoundrel; a vaguer term than
today)   12 **passion** emotional outburst   25 **keep his day** pay on
the exact day appointed

Salerio.   Marry, well rememb'red.
I reasoned° with a Frenchman yesterday,
Who told me, in the narrow seas° that part
The French and English there miscarried
30 A vessel of our country richly fraught.°
I thought upon Antonio when he told me,
And wished in silence that it were not his.

Solanio. You were best to tell Antonio what you hear.
Yet do not suddenly, for it may grieve him.

35 *Salerio.* A kinder gentleman treads not the earth.
I saw Bassanio and Antonio part.
Bassanio told him he would make some speed
Of his return; he answered, "Do not so.
Slubber° not business for my sake, Bassanio,
40 But stay the very riping of the time;
And for the Jew's bond which he hath of me,
Let it not enter in your mind of love.°
Be merry, and employ your chiefest thoughts
To courtship and such fair ostents° of love
45 As shall conveniently become you there."
And even there, his eye being big with tears,
Turning his face, he put his hand behind him,
And with affection wondrous sensible°
He wrung Bassanio's hand; and so they parted.

50 *Solanio.* I think he only loves the world for him.
I pray thee let us go and find him out,
And quicken his embracèd heaviness°
With some delight or other.

Salerio.   Do we so.   *Exeunt.*

---

27 **reasoned** talked   28 **narrow seas** English Channel   30 **fraught**
freighted   39 **Slubber** hurry over in a slovenly way   42 **mind of
love** loving thoughts (probably about both Antonio and Portia)
44 **ostents** shows, expressions   48 **affection wondrous sensible** won-
derfully strong emotion   52 **quicken his embracèd heaviness** lighten
the gloom which he has embraced

[Scene IX. *Belmont. Portia's house.*]

Enter Nerissa and a Servitor.

Nerissa. Quick, quick I pray thee, draw the curtain
    straight.°
    The Prince of Aragon hath ta'en his oath,
    And comes to his election° presently.°
    [*Flourish of cornets.*] *Enter Aragon, his Train, and
    Portia.*

Portia. Behold, there stand the caskets, noble Prince.
    If you choose that wherein I am contained,   5
    Straight shall our nuptial rites be solemnized;
    But if you fail, without more speech, my lord,
    You must be gone from hence immediately.

Aragon. I am enjoined by oath to observe three things:
    First, never to unfold to any one   10
    Which casket 'twas I chose; next, if I fail
    Of the right casket, never in my life
    To woo a maid in way of marriage;
    Lastly, if I do fail in fortune of my choice,
    Immediately to leave you and be gone.   15

Portia. To these injunctions everyone doth swear
    That comes to hazard for my worthless self.

Aragon. And so° have I addressed me.° Fortune now
    To my heart's hope! Gold, silver, and base lead.
    "Who chooseth me must give and hazard all he hath."   20
    You shall look fairer ere I give or hazard.
    What says the golden chest? Ha, let me see!
    "Who chooseth me shall gain what many men desire."

II.ix.1 **straight** at once   3 **election** choice   3 **presently** at this present moment, instantly   18 **so** on these terms   18 **have I addressed
me** I have addressed myself (to this affair)

What many men desire—that "many" may be meant
25 By° the fool multitude that choose by show,
Not learning more than the fond° eye doth teach,
Which pries not to th' interior, but like the martlet°
Builds in the weather on the outward wall,
Even in the force and road of casualty.°
30 I will not choose what many men desire,
Because I will not jump with° common spirits
And rank me with the barbarous multitudes.
Why then, to thee, thou silver treasure house!
Tell me once more what title thou dost bear.
35 "Who chooseth me shall get as much as he deserves."
And well said too, for who shall go about
To cozen° fortune, and be honorable
Without the stamp of merit? Let none presume
To wear an undeservèd dignity.
40 O that estates, degrees,° and offices°
Were not derived corruptly, and that clear honor
Were purchased by the merit of the wearer!
How many then should cover° that stand bare!
How many be commanded that command;
45 How much low peasantry would then be gleanèd°
From the true seed of honor!° And how much honor
Picked from the chaff and ruin of the times
To be new varnished.° Well, but to my choice.
"Who chooseth me shall get as much as he deserves."
50 I will assume desert. Give me a key for this,
And instantly unlock my fortunes here.

                              [*He opens the silver casket.*]

Portia. Too long a pause for that which you find there.°

25 By with regard to   26 fond foolish   27 martlet martin, a bird
29 in . . . casualty exposed to the tyrannic force of mischance and
lying in the open road   31 jump with accord with   37 cozen cheat
40 degrees ranks   40 offices official positions   43 cover wear hats,
in sign of authority   45 gleanèd picked out, as in gleaning grain
(cf. line 47, "Picked from the chaff")   46 seed of honor descendants
of ancient nobility   48 To be new varnished to have the luster of
their family restored   52 Too . . . there (probably an aside)

Aragon. What's here? The portrait of a blinking idiot
Presenting me a schedule!° I will read it.
How much unlike art thou to Portia!
How much unlike my hopes and my deservings!
"Who chooseth me shall have as much as he
  deserves."
Did I deserve no more than a fool's head?
Is that my prize? Are my deserts no better?   55

Portia. To offend and judge are distinct offices,   60
And of opposèd natures.°

Aragon.   What is here?
              "The fire° seven times tried this;°
              Seven times tried that judgment is
              That did never choose amiss.
              Some there be that shadows kiss;   65
              Such have but a shadow's bliss.
              There be fools alive iwis,°
              Silvered o'er,° and so was this.
              Take what wife you will to bed,
              I° will ever be your head.   70
              So be gone; you are sped."°
Still more fool I shall appear
By the time I linger here.
With one fool's head I came to woo,
But I go away with two.   75
Sweet, adieu. I'll keep my oath,
Patiently to bear my wroath.° [*Exit with his Train.*]

Portia. Thus hath the candle singed the moth.
O these deliberate fools! When they do choose,
They have the wisdom by their wit° to lose.   80

Nerissa. The ancient saying is no heresy:
Hanging and wiving goes by destiny.

Portia. Come draw the curtain, Nerissa.

54 schedule scroll   60–61 To offend . . . natures the offender is not
to judge himself   62 fire (pronounced fí-er)   62 this i.e., the silver
of the casket   67 iwis certainly   68 Silvered o'er i.e., with the gray
hair usually associated with wisdom   70 I "the blinking idiot" of
line 53   71 you are sped you have achieved your fortune   77 wroath
heavy lot (?)   80 wit cleverness

Enter Messenger.

Messenger. Where is my lady?

Portia.   Here. What would my lord?°

85 *Messenger.* Madam, there is alighted at your gate
       A young Venetian, one that comes before
       To signify th' approaching of his lord,
       From whom he bringeth sensible regreets,°
       To wit, besides commends and courteous breath,
90   Gifts of rich value. Yet I have not seen°
       So likely° an ambassador of love.
       A day in April never came so sweet
       To show how costly° summer was at hand,
       As this forespurrer° comes before his lord.

95 *Portia.* No more, I pray thee. I am half afeard
       Thou wilt say anon he is some kin to thee,
       Thou spend'st such high-day wit° in praising him.
       Come, come, Nerissa, for I long to see
       Quick Cupid's post° that comes so mannerly.

100 *Nerissa.* Bassanio, Lord Love,° if thy will it be!

                                        Exeunt.

---

84 **What would my lord?** (a gay, jesting retort to the messenger's
"my lady") 88 **sensible regreets** a quibble: greetings (1) expressing
strong feeling, and (2) conveying tangible gifts 90 **yet I have not
seen** not yet have I seen 91 **likely** promising 93 **costly** rich, plente-
ous 94 **forespurrer** advance messenger (one who spurs his horse
ahead of his party) 97 **high-day wit** imagination befitting a festive
occasion 99 **post** messenger 100 **Lord Love** god of love

[ACT III

Scene I. *Venice. A street.*]

[Enter] Solanio and Salerio.

Solanio. Now what news on the Rialto?

Salerio. Why, yet it lives there unchecked° that Antonio
hath a ship of rich lading wracked on the narrow
seas°—the Goodwins° I think they call the place—
a very dangerous flat, and fatal, where the carcasses   5
of many a tall ship lie buried as they say, if my gos-
sip° Report be an honest woman of her word.

Solanio. I would she were as lying a gossip in that, as
ever knapped° ginger or made her neighbors believe
she wept for the death of a third husband. But it is   10
true, without any slips of prolixity° or crossing the
plain highway of talk,° that the good Antonio, the
honest Antonio—O that I had a title good enough to
keep his name company!—

Salerio. Come, the full stop.°   15

Solanio. Ha, what sayest thou? Why the end is, he hath
lost a ship.

Salerio. I would it might prove the end of his losses.

III.i.2 **it lives there unchecked** it is reported without dispute   3–4
narrow seas English Channel   4 **Goodwins** Goodwin Sands, a shoal
6–7 **gossip** talkative comrade   9 **knapped** snapped, bit   11 **slips of
prolixity** long-winded lies   11–12 **crossing . . . talk** going counter to
honest speech   15 **Come, the full stop** come to the end of your
sentence

Solanio. Let me say Amen betimes,° lest the devil cross
20   my prayer, for here he comes in the likeness of a Jew.

Enter Shylock.

How now, Shylock? What news among the merchants?

Shylock. You knew, none so well, none so well as you,
of my daughter's flight.

25   *Salerio.* That's certain. I for my part knew the tailor that
made the wings she flew withal.

Solanio. And Shylock for his own part knew the bird
was fledge,° and then it is the complexion° of them
all to leave the dam.

30   *Shylock.* She is damned for it.

Salerio. That's certain, if the devil may be her judge.

Shylock. My own flesh and blood to rebel!

Solanio. Out upon it, old carrion! Rebels it° at these
years?

35   *Shylock.* I say my daughter is my flesh and my blood.

Salerio. There is more difference between thy flesh and
hers than between jet and ivory, more between your
bloods than there is between red wine and Rhenish.
But tell us, do you hear whether Antonio have had
40   any loss at sea or no?

Shylock. There I have another bad match! A bankrout,° a prodigal, who dare scarce show his head on
the Rialto, a beggar that was used to come so smug°
upon the mart! Let him look to his bond. He was
45   wont to call me usurer. Let him look to his bond. He
was wont to lend money for a Christian cursy.° Let
him look to his bond.

19 betimes promptly   **28 fledge** feathered, able to fly   **28 complexion** natural disposition   **33 Rebels it** (a contemptuous pun on "flesh
and blood" in the sense of fleshly desire)   **41-42 bankrout** bankrupt
43 smug well-groomed   **46 cursy** courtesy

Salerio. Why, I am sure if he forfeit thou wilt not take his flesh. What's that good for?

Shylock. To bait fish withal. If it will feed nothing else, 50 it will feed my revenge. He hath disgraced me, and hind'red me half a million, laughed at my losses, mocked at my gains, scorned my nation, thwarted my bargains, cooled my friends, heated mine ene-mies—and what's his reason? I am a Jew. Hath not 55 a Jew eyes? Hath not a Jew hands, organs, dimen-sions,° senses, affections,° passions?—fed with the same food, hurt with the same weapons, subject to the same diseases, healed by the same means, warmed and cooled by the same winter and summer as a 60 Christian is? If you prick us, do we not bleed? If you tickle us, do we not laugh? If you poison us, do we not die? And if you wrong us, shall we not revenge? If we are like you in the rest, we will resemble you in that. If a Jew wrong a Christian, what is his humil- 65 ity?° Revenge! If a Christian wrong a Jew, what should his sufferance be by Christian example? Why revenge! The villainy you teach me I will execute, and it shall go hard but I will better the instruction.

Enter a Man from Antonio.

[*Man.*] Gentlemen, my master Antonio is at his house, 70 and desires to speak with you both.

Salerio. We have been up and down to seek him.

Enter Tubal.

Solanio. Here comes another of the tribe. A third can-not be matched, unless the devil himself turn Jew.
     Exeunt Gentlemen [Solanio, Salerio, and Man].

Shylock. How now, Tubal! What news from Genoa? 75 Hast thou found my daughter?

56–57 dimensions limbs, features, etc.   57 affections feelings   65–66 what is his humility? what does his Christian humility amount to?

Tubal. I often came where I did hear of her, but cannot find her.

Shylock. Why there, there, there, there! A diamond
80   gone cost me two thousand ducats in Frankford! The
curse never fell upon our nation till now; I never felt
it till now. Two thousand ducats in that, and other
precious, precious jewels. I would my daughter were
dead at my foot, and the jewels in her ear! Would she
85   were hearsed at my foot, and the ducats in her coffin!
No news of them? Why, so! And I know not what's
spent in the search. Why thou loss upon loss—the
thief gone with so much, and so much to find the
thief!—and no satisfaction, no revenge, nor no ill
90   luck stirring but what lights o' my shoulders, no sighs
but o' my breathing, no tears but o' my shedding.

Tubal. Yes, other men have ill luck too. Antonio, as I
heard in Genoa—

Shylock. What, what, what? Ill luck, ill luck?

95 *Tubal.* Hath an argosy cast away coming from Tripolis.

Shylock. I thank God, I thank God! Is it true, is it true?

Tubal. I spoke with some of the sailors that escaped the
wrack.

Shylock. I thank thee, good Tubal. Good news, good
100   news! Ha, ha! Heard in Genoa?

Tubal. Your daughter spent in Genoa, as I heard, one
night fourscore ducats.

Shylock. Thou stick'st a dagger in me. I shall never see
my gold again. Fourscore ducats at a sitting, fourscore
105   ducats!

Tubal. There came divers of Antonio's creditors in my
company to Venice that swear he cannot choose but
break.°

108 break go bankrupt

Shylock. I am very glad of it. I'll plague him; I'll torture
him. I am glad of it. *110*

Tubal. One of them showed me a ring that he had of
your daughter for a monkey.

Shylock. Out upon her! Thou torturest me, Tubal. It
was my turquoise; I had it of Leah° when I was a
bachelor. I would not have given it for a wilderness *115*
of monkeys.

Tubal. But Antonio is certainly undone.

Shylock. Nay, that's true, that's very true. Go, Tubal,
fee me an officer;° bespeak° him a fortnight before.
I will have the heart of him if he forfeit, for were he *120*
out of Venice I can make what merchandise° I will.
Go, Tubal, and meet me at our synagogue; go, good
Tubal; at our synagogue, Tubal. *Exeunt.*

[Scene II. *Belmont. Portia's house.*]

*Enter Bassanio, Portia, Gratiano, [Nerissa,] and
all their Trains.*

Portia. I pray you tarry; pause a day or two
Before you hazard, for in choosing wrong
I lose your company. Therefore forbear awhile.
There's something tells me (but it is not love)
I would not lose you; and you know yourself *5*
Hate counsels not in such a quality.°
But lest you should not understand me well—
And yet a maiden hath no tongue but thought—
I would detain you here some month or two
Before you venture for me. I could teach you *10*

114 Leah Shylock's wife   119 officer (to arrest Antonio)   119 be-
speak engage   121 merchandise wealth III.ii.6 in such a quality in
such a manner of speech as I am using to you

How to choose right, but then I am forsworn.
So will I never be. So may you miss me.
But if you do, you'll make me wish a sin—
That I had been forsworn. Beshrow° your eyes!
15 They have o'erlooked° me and divided me;
One half of me is yours, the other half yours—
Mine own I would say; but if mine then yours,
And so all yours! O these naughty° times
Puts bars between the owners and their rights!
20 And so, though yours, not yours. Prove it so,°
Let fortune go to hell for it, not I.
I speak too long, but 'tis to peize° the time,
To eche° it and to draw it out in length,
To stay you from election.

Bassanio.   Let me choose,
25 For as I am, I live upon the rack.°

Portia. Upon the rack, Bassanio? Then confess
What treason there is mingled with your love.°

Bassanio. None but that ugly treason of mistrust,
Which makes me fear th' enjoying of my love.
30 There may as well be amity and life
'Tween snow and fire, as treason and my love.

Portia. Ay, but I fear you speak upon the rack,
Where men enforcèd° do speak anything.

Bassanio. Promise me life, and I'll confess the truth.

Portia. Well then, confess and live.

35 *Bassanio.*   Confess and love
Had been the very sum of my confession!
O happy torment, when my torturer
Doth teach me answers for deliverance.°

---

14 Beshrow curse (but a playful word)   15 o'erlooked bewitched
18 naughty wicked   20 Prove it so if it should prove so   22 peize
weigh down, hence retard   23 eche eke out, i.e., lengthen   25 rack
instrument of torture, on which the body was pulled with great
force, often breaking the joints; used to force confessions, especially
in trials for treason   27 What treason . . . love (spoken playfully)
33 enforcèd compelled (by torture)   38 answers for deliverance
answers to free me from torture

But let me to my fortune and the caskets.

Portia. Away then! I am locked in one of them;   40
If you do love me, you will find me out.
Nerissa and the rest, stand all aloof.
Let music sound while he doth make his choice;
Then if he lose he makes a swanlike end,°
Fading in music. That the comparison   45
May stand more proper, my eye shall be the stream
And wat'ry deathbed for him. He may win;
And what is music then? Then music is
Even as the flourish° when true subjects bow
To a new-crownèd monarch. Such it is   50
As are those dulcet sounds in break of day,
That creep into the dreaming bridegroom's ear
And summon him to marriage. Now he goes,
With no less presence,° but with much more love,
Than young Alcides,° when he did redeem   55
The virgin tribute° paid by howling Troy
To the sea monster. I stand for sacrifice;
The rest aloof are the Dardanian wives,
With blearèd visages come forth to view
The issue of th' exploit. Go, Hercules!   60
Live thou,° I live. With much, much more dismay°
I view the fight than thou that mak'st the fray.°

*A song the whilst Bassanio comments on the
caskets to himself.*

> Tell me where is fancy° bred,
> Or in the heart, or in the head?
> How begot, how nourishèd?   65
>   Reply, reply.
> It is engend'red in the eyes,

---

44 **swanlike end** an end like the swan's (who was supposed never to
sing until it sang enchantingly at its death)   49 **flourish** fanfare of
trumpets   54 **presence** noble bearing   55 **Alcides** Hercules   56 **virgin tribute** Hesione, Priam's sister, who was offered as a divine sacrifice to be devoured by a sea monster; Hercules slew the monster and
saved her   61 **Live thou** if thou live   61 **dismay** alarm and terror
62 **fray** combat   63 **fancy** love based only on the senses, especially
the sight

With gazing fed, and fancy dies
In the cradle where it lies.
70   Let us all ring fancy's knell.
I'll begin it—Ding, dong, bell.

All.   Ding, dong, bell.

Bassanio. So° may the outward shows be least
themselves;°
The world is still° deceived with ornament.
75   In law, what plea so tainted and corrupt,
But being seasoned with a gracious voice,
Obscures the show of evil? In religion,
What damnèd error but some sober brow
Will bless it, and approve it with a text,°
80   Hiding the grossness with fair ornament?
There is no vice so simple but assumes
Some mark of virtue on his outward parts.
How many cowards whose hearts are all as false
As stairs of sand, wear yet upon their chins
85   The beards of Hercules and frowning Mars,
Who inward searched, have livers white as milk!°
And these assume but valor's excrement°
To render them redoubted.° Look on beauty,
And you shall see 'tis purchased by the weight,
90   Which therein works a miracle in nature,
Making them lightest° that wear most of it:
So are those crispèd° snaky golden locks,
Which maketh such wanton° gambols with the wind
Upon supposèd fairness, often known
95   To be the dowry° of a second head,
The skull that bred them in the sepulcher.
Thus ornament is but the guilèd° shore
To a most dangerous sea, the beauteous scarf

---

73 So thus   73 least themselves least like what they really are
74 still continually   79 approve it with a text prove it by a biblical text   86 livers white as milk (a pale liver supposedly caused
cowardice)   87 excrement excrescence, outer appearance   88 redoubted dreaded   91 lightest (a pun on "light" in the sense of unchaste)   92 crispèd curled   93 wanton playful   95 dowry gift of
property, i.e., hair from a dead person's head   97 guilèd full of
guile, treacherous

Veiling an Indian° beauty; in a word,
The seeming truth which cunning times put on   *100*
To entrap the wisest. Therefore then, thou gaudy
    gold,
Hard food for Midas, I will none of thee;
Nor none of thee, thou pale and common drudge°
'Tween man and man. But thou, thou meager° lead
Which rather threaten'st than dost promise aught,   *105*
Thy paleness moves me more than eloquence;
And here choose I. Joy be the consequence!

Portia. [*Aside*] How all the other passions fleet to air,
As doubtful thoughts, and rash-embraced despair,
And shudd'ring fear, and green-eyed jealousy.   *110*
O love, be moderate, allay thy ecstasy,
In measure rain thy joy, scant° this excess!
I feel too much thy blessing. Make it less
For fear I surfeit.°

Bassanio. [*Opening the leaden casket*] What find I here?
Fair Portia's counterfeit!° What demigod°   *115*
Hath come so near creation? Move these eyes?
Or whether, riding on the balls of mine,°
Seem they in motion? Here are severed lips
Parted with sugar breath; so sweet a bar°
Should sunder such sweet friends.° Here in her hairs   *120*
The painter plays the spider, and hath woven
A golden mesh t' entrap the hearts of men
Faster° than gnats in cobwebs. But her eyes—
How could he see to do them? Having made one,
Methinks it should have power to steal both his   *125*
And leave itself unfurnished.° Yet look how far

99 **Indian** East Indian, hence dusky   103 **pale and common drudge**
pale hack worker, i.e., silver   104 **meager** poverty-stricken, of slight
value   112 **scant** lessen   114 **surfeit** grow sick with too much, i.e.,
too much joy   115 **counterfeit** image   115 **demigod** i.e., half-divine
painter   117 **the balls of mine** my eyeballs   119 **so sweet a bar** i.e.,
Portia's breath   120 **sweet friends** i.e., her lips   123 **Faster** tighter
126 **unfurnished** not provided with its mate (since the picture of the
first eye has taken away both of the painter's eyes)

The substance° of my praise doth wrong this shadow°
In underprizing it, so far this shadow
Doth limp behind the substance. Here's the scroll,
130   The continent and summary° of my fortune.

"You that choose not by the view
Chance as fair,° and choose as true.
Since this fortune falls to you,
Be content and seek no new.
135   If you be well pleased with this
And hold your fortune for your bliss,
Turn you where your lady is,
And claim her with a loving kiss."

A gentle° scroll. Fair lady, by your leave.
                                    [Kisses her.]
140   I come by note,° to give and to receive.
Like one of two contending in a prize,°
That thinks he hath done well in people's eyes,
Hearing applause and universal shout,
Giddy in spirit, still gazing in a doubt
145   Whether those peals of praise be his° or no—
So, thrice-fair lady, stand I even so,
As doubtful whether what I see be true,
Until confirmed, signed, ratified by you.

Portia. You see me, Lord Bassanio, where I stand,
150   Such as I am. Though for myself alone
I would not be ambitious in my wish
To wish myself much better, yet for you
I would be trebled twenty times myself,
A thousand times more fair, ten thousand times more
    rich,
155   That only to stand high in your account,°
I might in virtues, beauties, livings,° friends,

127, 129 The substance Portia herself   127, 128 this shadow her picture   130 The continent and summary that which contains and sums
up   132 Chance as fair have as fair fortune   139 gentle courteous,
well-bred   140 by note according to instructions (in lines 137–38)
141 prize contest for a prize, as in a tournament   145 his intended
for him   155 account esteem, regard   156 livings possessions

Exceed account.° But the full sum of me
Is sum of something—which, to term in gross,°
Is an unlessoned girl, unschooled, unpracticed;
Happy in this, she is not yet so old   160
But she may learn; happier than this,
She is not bred so dull but she can learn;
Happiest of all, is that her gentle spirit
Commits itself to yours to be directed,
As from her lord, her governor, her king.   165
Myself, and what is mine, to you and yours
Is now converted.° But now° I was the lord
Of this fair mansion, master of my servants,
Queen o'er myself; and even now, but now,
This house, these servants, and this same myself   170
Are yours, my lord's. I give them with this ring,
Which when you part from, lose, or give away,
Let it presage° the ruin of your love
And be my vantage to exclaim on° you.

Bassanio. Madam, you have bereft me of all words.   175
Only my blood speaks to you in my veins,
And there is such confusion in my powers
As, after some oration fairly spoke
By a belovèd prince,° there doth appear
Among the buzzing pleasèd multitude;   180
Where every something being blent together
Turns to a wild of nothing, save of joy
Expressed and not expressed. But when this ring
Parts from this finger, then parts life from hence!
O then be bold to say Bassanio's dead!   185

Nerissa. My lord and lady, it is now our time,
That have stood by and seen our wishes prosper,
To cry "good joy." Good joy, my lord and lady!

---

157 **account** computation   158 **term in gross** describe in broad terms
167 **converted** changed, i.e., made yours   167 **But now** only now
173 **presage** foretell   174 **vantage to exclaim on** opportunity to cry
out against (lines 173–74 spoken playfully)   179 **prince** (a feminine
as well as a masculine noun; hence suitably applied to Portia)

Gratiano. My Lord Bassanio, and my gentle lady,
190   I wish you all the joy that you can wish—
For I am sure you can wish none from° me;
And when your honors mean to solemnize
The bargain of your faith, I do beseech you
Even at that time I may be married too.

195 *Bassanio.* With all my heart, so° thou canst get a wife.

Gratiano. I thank your lordship, you have got me one.
My eyes, my lord, can look as swift as yours:
You saw the mistress, I beheld the maid.
You loved, I loved; for intermission°
200   No more pertains to me, my lord, than you.
Your fortune stood upon the caskets there,
And so did mine too, as the matter falls;
For wooing here until I sweat again,°
And swearing till my very roof° was dry
205   With oaths of love, at last—if promise last°—
I got a promise of this fair one here
To have her love, provided that your fortune
Achieved her mistress.

Portia.   Is this true, Nerissa?

Nerissa. Madam, it is, so you stand pleased withal.

210 *Bassanio.* And do you, Gratiano, mean good faith?

Gratiano. Yes, faith, my lord.

Bassanio. Our feast shall be much honored in your
marriage.

Gratiano. We'll play with them the first boy for a
thousand ducats.

215 *Nerissa.* What, and stake down?°

Gratiano. No, we shall ne'er win at that sport, and stake
down.

---

191 **from** away from   195 **so** provided   199 **intermission** pausing
203 **again** i.e., again and again   204 **roof** roof of the mouth   205 **if
promise last** if her promise holds   215 **stake down** a betting term
(with an off-color pun)

But who comes here? Lorenzo and his infidel!°
What, and my old Venetian friend Salerio!

*Enter Lorenzo, Jessica, and Salerio, a Messenger
from Venice.*

Bassanio. Lorenzo and Salerio, welcome hither,   220
If that the youth of my new int'rest° here
Have power to bid you welcome. By your leave,
I bid my very friends and countrymen,
Sweet Portia, welcome.

Portia.   So do I, my lord.   225
They are entirely welcome.

Lorenzo. I thank your honor. For my part, my lord,
My purpose was not to have seen you here,
But meeting with Salerio by the way,
He did entreat me past all saying nay
To come with him along.

Salerio.   I did, my lord,   230
And I have reason for it. Signior Antonio
Commends him to you.°   [*Gives Bassanio a letter.*]

Bassanio.   Ere I ope his letter,
I pray you tell me how my good friend doth.

Salerio. Not sick, my lord, unless it be in mind,
Nor well, unless in mind. His letter there   235
Will show you his estate.°   *Open the letter.*

Gratiano. Nerissa, cheer yond stranger; bid her
        welcome.
Your hand, Salerio. What's the news from Venice?
How doth that royal merchant,° good Antonio?
I know he will be glad of our success;
We are the Jasons, we have won the Fleece.   240

218 **infidel** one who lacks the true faith (Gratiano applies the term
playfully to Jessica; cf. II.vi.51) 221 **int'rest** claim 232 **Commends him to you** sends you his best wishes 236 **estate** state, condition 239 **royal merchant** merchant prince

Salerio. I would you had won the fleece° that he hath
    lost!

Portia. There are some shrowd° contents in yond same
    paper
    That steals the color from Bassanio's cheek:
243   Some dear friend dead, else nothing in the world
    Could turn so much the constitution
    Of any constant man. What, worse and worse?
    With leave, Bassanio——I am half yourself,
    And I must freely have the half of anything
    That this same paper brings you.

250 *Bassanio.*   O sweet Portia,
    Here are a few of the unpleasant'st words
    That ever blotted paper! Gentle lady,
    When I did first impart my love to you,
    I freely told you all the wealth I had
255   Ran in my veins——I was a gentleman.
    And then I told you true; and yet, dear lady,
    Rating myself at nothing, you shall see
    How much I was a braggart. When I told you
    My state° was nothing, I should then have told you
260   That I was worse than nothing; for indeed
    I have engaged° myself to a dear friend,
    Engaged my friend to his mere° enemy
    To feed my means. Here is a letter, lady,
    The paper as the body of my friend,
265   And every word in it a gaping wound
    Issuing lifeblood. But is it true, Salerio?
    Hath all his ventures failed? What, not one hit?
    From Tripolis, from Mexico and England,
    From Lisbon, Barbary, and India,
270   And not one vessel scape the dreadful touch
    Of merchant-marring rocks?

Salerio.   Not one, my lord.
    Besides, it should appear that if he had
    The present° money to discharge° the Jew,

---

242 **fleece** (pun on "fleets")   243 **shrowd** evil, grievous; literally
"cursed"   259 **state** estate, fortune   261 **engaged** pledged   262
mere absolute   273 **present** ready   273 **discharge** pay

He would not take it. Never did I know
A creature that did bear the shape of man
So keen and greedy to confound° a man.   275
He plies the Duke at morning and at night,
And doth impeach the freedom of the state°
If they deny him justice. Twenty merchants,
The Duke himself, and the magnificoes
Of greatest port° have all persuaded with him,   280
But none can drive him from the envious° plea
Of forfeiture, of justice, and his bond.

Jessica. When I was with him, I have heard him swear
To Tubal and to Chus, his countrymen,   285
That he would rather have Antonio's flesh
Than twenty times the value of the sum
That he did owe him; and I know, my lord,
If law, authority, and power deny not,
It will go hard with poor Antonio.   290

Portia. Is it your dear friend that is thus in trouble?

Bassanio. The dearest friend to me, the kindest man,
The best-conditioned° and unwearied spirit
In doing courtesies, and one in whom
The ancient Roman honor more appears   295
Than any that draws breath in Italy.

Portia. What sum owes he the Jew?

Bassanio. For me, three thousand ducats.

Portia.   What, no more?
Pay him six thousand, and deface° the bond.
Double six thousand and then treble that,   300
Before a friend of this description
Shall lose a hair through Bassanio's fault.
First go with me to church and call me wife,
And then away to Venice to your friend!
For never shall you lie by Portia's side   305

---

276 **confound** ruin, destroy   278 **impeach . . . state** charge that
Venice is no free state   280–81 **magnificoes/Of greatest port** nobles
of highest dignity   282 **envious** malignant   293 **The best-condi-
tioned** of the best disposition   299 **deface** destroy

With an unquiet soul. You shall have gold
To pay the petty debt twenty times over;
When it is paid, bring your true friend along.
My maid Nerissa and myself meantime
310 Will live as maids and widows. Come away!
For you shall hence° upon your wedding day.
Bid your friends welcome, show a merry cheer;
Since you are dear bought, I will love you dear.
But let me hear the letter of your friend.

315 [*Bassanio.* (*Reads*)] "Sweet Bassanio, my ships have
all miscarried, my creditors grow cruel, my estate is
very low, my bond to the Jew is forfeit. And since in
paying it, it is impossible I should live, all debts are
cleared between you and I if I might but see you at
320 my death. Notwithstanding, use your pleasure. If
your love do not persuade you to come, let not my
letter."

Portia. O love, dispatch all business and be gone!

Bassanio. Since I have your good leave to go away,
325 I will make haste; but till I come again
No bed shall e'er be guilty of my stay,
Nor rest be interposer 'twixt us twain.   *Exeunt.*

[Scene III. *Venice. A street.*]

Enter [*Shylock*] *the Jew and Solanio and Antonio
and the Jailer.*

Shylock. Jailer, look to him. Tell not me of mercy.
This is the fool that lent out money gratis.
Jailer, look to him.

Antonio.   Hear me yet, good Shylock.

Shylock. I'll have my bond! Speak not against my bond!

311 shall hence must go hence

I have sworn an oath that I will have my bond.   *5*
Thou call'dst me dog before thou hadst a cause,
But since I am a dog, beware my fangs.
The Duke shall grant me justice. I do wonder,
Thou naughty° jailer, that thou art so fond°
To come abroad with him at his request.   *10*

Antonio. I pray thee hear me speak.

Shylock. I'll have my bond. I will not hear thee speak.
I'll have my bond, and therefore speak no more.
I'll not be made a soft and dull-eyed fool,
To shake the head, relent, and sigh, and yield   *15*
To Christian intercessors. Follow not.
I'll have no speaking; I will have my bond.

                            Exit Jew.

Solanio. It is the most impenetrable cur
That ever kept° with men.

Antonio.   Let him alone;
I'll follow him no more with bootless° prayers.   *20*
He seeks my life. His reason well I know:
I oft delivered from his forfeitures°
Many that have at times made moan to me.
Therefore he hates me.

Solanio.   I am sure the Duke
Will never grant this forfeiture to hold.   *25*

Antonio. The Duke cannot deny the course of law;
For the commodity° that strangers° have
With us in Venice, if it be denied,
Will much impeach the justice of the state,
Since that the trade and profit of the city   *30*
Consisteth of all nations. Therefore go.
These griefs° and losses have so bated° me
That I shall hardly spare a pound of flesh
Tomorrow to my bloody creditor.

III.iii.9 **naughty** wicked   9 **fond** foolish   19 **kept** dwelt   20 **bootless** unavailing   22 **forfeitures** penalties that he could have legally exacted   27 **commodity** commercial advantage   27 **strangers** foreigners   32 **griefs** pains   32 **bated** reduced

35 Well, jailer, on. Pray God Bassanio come
    To see me pay his debt, and then I care not! *Exeunt.*

[Scene IV. *Belmont. Portia's house.*]

*Enter Portia, Nerissa, Lorenzo, Jessica, and
    [Balthasar,] a Man of Portia's.*

Lorenzo. Madam, although I speak it in your presence,
    You have a noble and a true conceit°
    Of godlike amity,° which appears most strongly
    In bearing thus the absence of your lord.
5   But if you knew to whom you show this honor,
    How true a gentleman you send relief,
    How dear a lover° of my lord your husband,
    I know you would be prouder of the work
    Than customary bounty can enforce you.°

10 *Portia.* I never did repent for doing good,
    Nor shall not now; for in companions
    That do converse and waste° the time together,
    Whose souls do bear an egal° yoke of love,
    There must be needs a like proportion
15 Of lineaments, of manners, and of spirit;
    Which makes me think that this Antonio,
    Being the bosom lover of my lord,
    Must needs be like my lord. If it be so,
    How little is the cost I have bestowed
20 In purchasing° the semblance° of my soul
    From out the state of hellish cruelty!
    This comes too near the praising of myself;

III.iv.2 **conceit** idea, conception   3 **amity** friendship   7 **lover** friend
8–9 **prouder . . . you** prouder of this action than even your habitual
kindness can make you   12 **converse and waste** associate and spend
13 **egal** equal   20 **purchasing** gaining   20 **semblance** likeness (Portia
refers to the old idea that a genuine friend or lover is a second self.
Antonio is like Bassanio, and therefore like Portia)

Therefore no more of it. Hear other things:
Lorenzo, I commit into your hands
The husbandry° and manage of my house,   *25*
Until my lord's return. For mine own part,
I have toward heaven breathed a secret vow
To live in prayer and contemplation,
Only attended by Nerissa here,
Until her husband and my lord's return.   *30*
There is a monast'ry two miles off,
And there we will abide. I do desire you
Not to deny this imposition,°
The which my love and some necessity
Now lays upon you.

Lorenzo.   Madam, with all my heart;   *35*
I shall obey you in all fair commands.

Portia. My people do already know my mind,
And will acknowledge you and Jessica
In place of Lord Bassanio and myself.
So fare you well till we shall meet again.   *40*

Lorenzo. Fair thoughts and happy hours attend on you!

Jessica. I wish your ladyship all heart's content.

Portia. I thank you for your wish, and am well pleased
To wish it back on you. Fare you well, Jessica.
                          Exeunt [Jessica and Lorenzo].
Now, Balthasar,   *45*
As I have ever found thee honest-true,
So let me find thee still. Take this same letter,
And use thou all th' endeavor of a man
In speed to Padua. See thou render this
Into my cousin's hands, Doctor Bellario;   *50*
And look what° notes and garments he doth give
   thee
Bring them, I pray thee, with imagined speed°
Unto the tranect,° to the common ferry

---

25 husbandry care 33 imposition task that I impose 51 look
what whatever 52 imagined speed speed of imagination 53 tranect ferry

Which trades to Venice. Waste no time in words
55   But get thee gone. I shall be there before thee.

Balthasar. Madam, I go with all convenient speed.°
                                              [*Exit.*]

Portia. Come on, Nerissa; I have work in hand
That you yet know not of. We'll see our husbands
Before they think of us.

Nerissa.   Shall they see us?

60   *Portia.* They shall, Nerissa, but in such a habit°
That they shall think we are accomplishèd°
With that we lack. I'll hold thee any wager,
When we are both accoutered like young men,
I'll prove the prettier° fellow of the two,
65   And wear my dagger with the braver grace,°
And speak between the change of man and boy
With a reed° voice, and turn two mincing steps
Into a manly stride, and speak of frays
Like a fine bragging youth, and tell quaint° lies,
70   How honorable ladies sought my love,
Which I denying, they fell sick and died—
I could not do withal!° Then I'll repent,
And wish, for all that,° that I had not killed them.
And twenty of these puny lies I'll tell,
75   That men shall swear I have discontinued school
Above a twelvemonth. I have within my mind
A thousand raw tricks of these bragging Jacks,°
Which I will practice.

Nerissa.   Why, shall we turn to° men?

Portia. Fie, what a question's that,
80   If thou wert near a lewd° interpreter!

---

56 **convenient speed** speed suited (to this emergency)   60 **habit** garment, i.e., men's clothes   61 **accomplishèd** provided   64 **prettier** more dashing   65 **braver grace** finer masculine grace   67 **reed** high or squeaky, like the sound of a reed pipe   69 **quaint** clever and elaborate   72 **I could not do withal** I could not help it   73 **for all that** in spite of that   77 **Jacks** fellows   78 **turn to** turn into (with an off-color pun; cf. I.iii.78)   80 **lewd** bad

But come, I'll tell thee all my whole device
When I am in my coach, which stays for us
At the park gate; and therefore haste away,
For we must measure twenty miles today.   *Exeunt.*

[Scene V. *Belmont. A garden.*]

Enter [Launcelot the] Clown and Jessica.

Launcelot. Yes truly; for look you, the sins of the father
are to be laid upon the children.° Therefore, I promise you I fear you.° I was always plain with you, and
so now I speak my agitation° of the matter. Therefore be o' good cheer, for truly I think you are   *5*
damned. There is but one hope in it that can do you
any good, and that is but a kind of bastard hope
neither.

Jessica. And what hope is that, I pray thee?

Launcelot. Marry, you may partly hope that your fa-   *10*
ther got you not—that you are not the Jew's daughter.

Jessica. That were a kind of bastard hope indeed! So°
the sins of my mother should be visited upon me.

Launcelot. Truly then, I fear you are damned both by
father and mother. Thus when I shun Scylla your   *15*
father, I fall into Charybdis your mother. Well, you
are gone both ways.

Jessica. I shall be saved by my husband.° He hath
made me a Christian.

Launcelot. Truly, the more to blame he! We were   *20*

III.v.1–2 **sins . . . children** (see Exodus 20:5) 3 **fear you** fear for
you 4 **agitation** (blunder for "cogitation") 12 **So** thus 18 **saved
by my husband** (see 1 Corinthians 7:14)

Christians enow° before,° e'en as many as could well
live one by another.° This making of Christians will
raise the price of hogs; if we grow all to be pork-
eaters, we shall not shortly have a rasher° on the
23   coals for money.

Enter Lorenzo.

Jessica. I'll tell my husband, Launcelot, what you say.
Here he comes.

Lorenzo. I shall grow jealious° of you shortly, Launcelot, if you thus get my wife into corners.

30   *Jessica.* Nay, you need not fear us, Lorenzo. Launcelot
and I are out.° He tells me flatly there's no mercy
for me in heaven because I am a Jew's daughter; and
he says you are no good member of the commonwealth, for in converting Jews to Christians you raise
35   the price of pork.

Lorenzo. [*To Launcelot*] I shall answer that better to
the commonwealth than you can the getting up of
the Negro's belly. The Moor° is with child by you,
Launcelot!

40   *Launcelot.* It is much that the Moor should be more
than reason; but if she be less than an honest° woman, she is indeed more than I took her for.

Lorenzo. How every fool can play upon the word! I
think the best grace° of wit will shortly turn into
45   silence, and discourse grow commendable in none
only but parrots. Go in, sirrah; bid them prepare for
dinner.

Launcelot. That is done, sir. They have all stomachs.

---

21 **enow** enough   21 **before** before you turned Christian   22 **one
by another** one off another   24 **rasher** slice of bacon   28 **jealious**
jealous   31 **out** at odds   38 **Moor** (pronounced "more"; hence
Launcelot quibbles on "much," "more," and "Moor")   41 **honest**
chaste   44 **grace** virtue

Lorenzo. Goodly Lord, what a wit-snapper are you!
  Then bid them prepare dinner.   50

Launcelot. That is done too, sir. Only "cover"° is the
  word.

Lorenzo. Will you cover then, sir?

Launcelot. Not so, sir, neither! I know my duty.

Lorenzo. Yet more quarreling with occasion!° Wilt   55
  thou show the whole wealth of thy wit in an instant?
  I pray thee understand a plain man in his plain
  meaning: go to thy fellows, bid them cover the table,
  serve in the meat, and we will come in to dinner.

Launcelot. For the table,° sir, it shall be served in; for   60
  the meat, sir, it shall be covered;° for your coming
  in to dinner, sir, why let it be as humors and con-
  ceits° shall govern.   *Exit Clown* [*Launcelot*].

Lorenzo. O dear discretion,° how his words are suited!°
  The fool hath planted in his memory
  An army of good words; and I do know   65
  A many° fools that stand in better place,
  Garnished° like him, that for a tricksy word
  Defy the matter.° How cheer'st thou,° Jessica?
  And now, good sweet, say thy opinion—
  How dost thou like the Lord Bassanio's wife?   70

Jessica. Past all expressing. It is very meet
  The Lord Bassanio live an upright life,
  For having such a blessing in his lady,
  He finds the joys of heaven here on earth;
  And if on earth he do not merit it,   75

51 **cover** cover the table (Launcelot proceeds to quibble on "cover"
in the sense of "wear a hat")   55 **quarreling with occasion** caviling
at every opportunity   60 **table** (1) the piece of furniture (2) the meal
61 **covered** i.e., to be kept hot   62–63 **humors and conceits** fancies
and notions   64 **dear discretion** precious common sense   64 **suited**
fitted together (?) dressed up (?)   67 **A many** (an old idiom for a
large number)   68 **Garnished** decked out   69 **the matter** good sense
69 **How cheer'st thou** how is it with thee (the implication is that he
kisses her)

In reason he should never come to heaven.
Why, if two gods should play some heavenly match
And on the wager lay° two earthly women,
80   And Portia one, there must be something else°
Pawned with the other, for the poor rude world
Hath not her fellow.

Lorenzo.   Even such a husband
Hast thou of me as she is for a wife.

Jessica. Nay, but ask my opinion too of that!

85 *Lorenzo.* I will anon. First let us go to dinner.

Jessica. Nay, let me praise you while I have a stomach.°

Lorenzo. No, pray thee, let it serve for table-talk;
Then howsome'er° thou speak'st, 'mong other things
I shall digest it.

Jessica.   Well, I'll set you forth.°

                             Exit [with Lorenzo].

---

79 lay stake   **80 something else** i.e., to make the wager fair   **86 stomach** (a pun on "desire" [to praise you] and an "appetite" for dinner)   **88 howsome'er** however   **89 I'll set you forth** I'll give a fine account of you

[ACT IV

Scene I. *Venice. A court of justice.*]

Enter the Duke, the Magnificoes, Antonio,
Bassanio, [Salerio,] and Gratiano [with others].

Duke. What,° is Antonio here?

Antonio. Ready, so please your Grace.

Duke. I am sorry for thee. Thou art come to answer
  A stony adversary, an inhuman wretch,
  Uncapable of pity, void and empty   5
  From any dram° of mercy.

Antonio.   I have heard
  Your Grace hath ta'en great pains to qualify°
  His rigorous course; but since he stands obdurate,
  And that no lawful means can carry me
  Out of his envy's reach,° I do oppose   10
  My patience to his fury, and am armed
  To suffer with a quietness of spirit
  The very tyranny and rage° of his.

Duke. Go one, and call the Jew into the court.

Salerio. He is ready at the door; he comes, my lord.   13

IV.i.1 **What** why (interjection) 6 **dram** mite, drop (literally an
eighth of an ounce) 7 **qualify** moderate 10 **his envy's reach** the
reach of his malignant hate 13 **tyranny and rage** savagery and
passion

Enter Shylock.

Duke. Make room, and let him stand before our° face.
    Shylock, the world thinks, and I think so too,
    That thou but leadest this fashion of thy malice
    To the last hour of act; and then 'tis thought
20   Thou'lt show thy mercy and remorse° more strange°
    Than is thy strange° apparent cruelty;
    And where thou now exacts the penalty,
    Which is a pound of this poor merchant's flesh,
    Thou wilt not only loose° the forfeiture,
25   But touched with human gentleness and love,
    Forgive a moiety° of the principal,
    Glancing an eye of pity on his losses,
    That have of late so huddled on his back—
    Enow° to press a royal merchant° down
30   And pluck commiseration of his state
    From brassy bosoms and rough hearts of flint,
    From stubborn Turks and Tartars never trained
    To offices of tender courtesy.
    We all expect° a gentle° answer, Jew.

Shylock. I have possessed° your Grace of what I
35   purpose,
    And by our holy Sabbath have I sworn
    To have the due and forfeit of my bond.
    If you deny it, let the danger light
    Upon your charter and your city's freedom!°
40   You'll ask me why I rather choose to have
    A weight of carrion flesh than to receive
    Three thousand ducats. I'll not answer that,
    But say it is my humor. Is it answered?
    What if my house be troubled with a rat,
45   And I be pleased to give ten thousand ducats

---

16 **our** (the royal "we," appropriate in giving an order, but in the next line the Duke uses "I," the informal singular, suited for a personal appeal to Shylock's feelings)   20 **remorse** compassion   20 **strange** wonderful   21 **strange** astonishing   24 **loose** release   26 **moiety** portion   29 **Enow** enough   29 **royal merchant** merchant prince   34 **expect** await   34 **gentle** befitting a gentleman   35 **possessed** informed   38–39 **danger . . . freedom** (cf. III.iii.27–31)

To have it baned?° What, are you answered yet?
Some men there are love not a gaping pig,°
Some that are mad if they behold a cat,
And others, when the bagpipe sings i' th' nose,
Cannot contain their urine; for affection,°   50
Master of passion,° sways it to the mood
Of what it likes or loathes. Now for your answer:
As there is no firm reason to be rend'red
Why he cannot abide a gaping pig,
Why he a harmless necessary cat,   55
Why he° a woollen bagpipe, but of force°
Must yield to such inevitable shame°
As to offend, himself being offended;
So can I give no reason, nor I will not,
More than a lodged° hate and a certain° loathing   60
I bear Antonio, that I follow thus
A losing suit against him. Are you answered?

Bassanio. This is no answer, thou unfeeling man,
  To excuse the current of thy cruelty!

Shylock. I am not bound° to please thee with my
  answers.   65

Bassanio. Do all men kill the things they do not love?

Shylock. Hates any man the thing he would not kill?

Bassanio. Every offense is not a hate at first.

Shylock. What, wouldst thou have a serpent sting thee
  twice?

Antonio. I pray you think you question° with the Jew.   70
  You may as well go stand upon the beach

---

46 **baned** poisoned   47 **gaping pig** young roast pig, often served with
fruit in its open mouth (Shylock invokes the old theory of natural
antipathy to explain his hatred of Antonio, thus concealing the real
cause; cf. I.iii. 39–42)   50 **affection** natural sympathy or antipathy
51 **passion** powerful emotion   54–56 **he . . . he . . . he** (pronounced
with heavy emphasis; this man . . . that man . . . another)   56 **of
force** of necessity, against his will   57 **shame** (as in line 50, above)
60 **lodged** fixed   60 **certain** assured, steadfast   65 **bound** bound by
law   70 **think you question** remember you argue

And bid the main flood bate his° usual height;
You may as well use question with the wolf,
Why he hath made the ewe bleat for the lamb;
75   You may as well forbid the mountain pines
To wag their high tops and to make no noise
When they are fretten° with the gusts of heaven;
You may as well do anything most hard
As seek to soften that—than which what's harder?—
80   His Jewish heart. Therefore I do beseech you
Make no moe offers, use no farther means,
But with all brief and plain conveniency°
Let me have judgment, and the Jew his will.

Bassanio. For thy three thousand ducats here is six.

85   *Shylock.* If every ducat in six thousand ducats
Were in six parts, and every part a ducat,
I would not draw° them. I would have my bond.

Duke. How shalt thou hope for mercy, rend'ring none?

Shylock. What judgment shall I dread, doing no wrong?
90   You have among you many a purchased slave,
Which like your asses and your dogs and mules
You use in abject and in slavish parts,°
Because you bought them. Shall I say to you,
"Let them be free! Marry them to your heirs!
95   Why sweat they under burdens? Let their beds
Be made as soft as yours, and let their palates
Be seasoned with such viands"? You will answer,
"The slaves are ours." So do I answer you:
The pound of flesh which I demand of him
100 Is dearly bought, is mine, and I will have it.
If you deny me, fie upon your law!
There is no force in the decrees of Venice.
I stand for judgment. Answer; shall I have it?

Duke. Upon my power I may dismiss this court
105 Unless Bellario, a learned doctor

---

72 main flood bate his ocean at high tide reduce its   77 fretten
fretted   **82 brief and plain conveniency** suitable brevity and direct-
ness   **87 draw** take   **92 parts** duties

Whom I have sent for to determine this,
Come here today.

Salerio.   My lord, here stays without
A messenger with letters from the doctor,
New come from Padua.

Duke. Bring us the letters. Call the messenger.   *110*

Bassanio. Good cheer, Antonio! What, man, courage
    yet!
The Jew shall have my flesh, blood, bones, and all,
Ere thou shalt lose for me one drop of blood.

Antonio. I am a tainted wether° of the flock,
Meetest° for death. The weakest kind of fruit   *115*
Drops earliest to the ground, and so let me.
You cannot better be employed, Bassanio,
Than to live still, and write mine epitaph.

    Enter Nerissa [dressed like a Lawyer's Clerk].

Duke. Came you from Padua, from Bellario?

Nerissa. From both, my lord. Bellario greets your
    Grace.   [*Presents a letter.*]   *120*

Bassanio. Why dost thou whet thy knife so earnestly?

Shylock. To cut the forfeiture from that bankrout there.

Gratiano. Not on thy sole, but on thy soul, harsh Jew,
Thou mak'st thy knife keen; but no metal can—
No, not the hangman's° ax—bear° half the keenness   *125*
Of thy sharp envy.° Can no prayers pierce thee?

Shylock. No, none that thou hast wit enough to make.

Gratiano. O be thou damned, inexecrable° dog,
And for thy life let justice be accused!°
Thou almost mak'st me waver in my faith,   *130*

114 tainted wether infected ram   115 Meetest fittest   125 hangman's executioner's   125 bear have   126 envy malignant hate
128 inexecrable most execrable, detestable   129 And . . . accused
(a much debated line. Probably, "Let justice be accused because
you have been allowed to live so long")

To hold opinion with Pythagoras°
That souls of animals infuse themselves
Into the trunks of men. Thy currish spirit
Governed a wolf who, hanged for human slaughter,°
135   Even from the gallows did his fell° soul fleet,
And whilst thou layest in thy unhallowed dam,°
Infused itself in thee; for thy desires
Are wolvish, bloody, starved, and ravenous.

Shylock. Till thou canst rail the seal from off my bond,
140   Thou but offend'st thy lungs to speak so loud.
Repair thy wit, good youth, or it will fall
To cureless ruin.° I stand here for law.

Duke. This letter from Bellario doth commend
A young and learned doctor to our court.
Where is he?

145   *Nerissa.*   He attendeth here hard by
To know your answer whether you'll admit him.

Duke. With all my heart. Some three or four of you
Go give him courteous conduct to this place.
Meantime the court shall hear Bellario's letter.

150   [*Clerk. (Reads)*] "Your Grace shall understand that at
the receipt of your letter I am very sick; but in the
instant that your messenger came, in loving visita-
tion was with me a young doctor of Rome. His name
is Balthasar. I acquainted him with the cause in
155   controversy between the Jew and Antonio the
merchant. We turned o'er many books together.
He is furnished with my opinion which, bettered
with his own learning, the greatness whereof I cannot enough commend, comes with him at my impor-
160   tunity to fill up° your Grace's request in my stead.

---

131 **Pythagoras** Greek philosopher of the 6th century B.C. who
taught the doctrine of the transmigration of souls   134 **hanged for
human slaughter** (wolves, dogs, and other animals were sometimes
hanged for killing or attacking people; hence the phrase "hangdog
look")   135 **fell** fierce   136 **dam** mother of an animal, here a she-
wolf   141–42 **fall/To cureless ruin** i.e., like a house too long out
of repair   160 **fill up** satisfy

I beseech you let his lack of years be no impediment
to let° him lack a reverend estimation, for I never
knew so young a body with so old a head. I leave
him to your gracious acceptance, whose trial° shall
better publish his commendation." 165

*Enter Portia for Balthasar, [dressed like a Doctor
of Laws].*

Duke. You hear the learn'd Bellario, what he writes;
    And here, I take it, is the doctor come.
    Give me your hand. Come you from old Bellario?

Portia. I did, my lord.

Duke.   You are welcome; take your place.
    Are you acquainted with the difference° 170
    That holds this present question° in the court?

Portia. I am informèd throughly° of the cause.°
    Which is the merchant here? And which the Jew?

Duke. Antonio and old Shylock, both stand forth.

Portia. Is your name Shylock?

Shylock.   Shylock is my name. 175

Portia. Of a strange° nature is the suit you follow,
    Yet in such rule that° the Venetian law
    Cannot impugn you as you do proceed.
    [*To Antonio*] You stand within his danger,° do you
        not?

Antonio. Ay, so he says.

Portia.   Do you confess the bond? 180

Antonio. I do.

Portia.   Then must the Jew be merciful.

---

162 **to let** to cause   164 **trial** conduct when brought to the test
170 **difference** dispute   171 **question** case under judicial examination
172 **throughly** thoroughly   172 **cause** case   176 **strange** astonishing   177 **in such rule that** within the rule so that   179 **danger**
power to harm

Shylock. On what compulsion must I? Tell me that.

Portia. The quality of mercy is not strained;°
It droppeth as the gentle rain from heaven
185   Upon the place beneath. It is twice blest;
It blesseth him that gives and him that takes.
'Tis mightiest in the mightiest; it becomes
The thronèd monarch better than his crown.
His scepter shows the force of temporal power,
190   The attribute to awe and majesty,
Wherein doth sit the dread and fear of kings;
But mercy is above this scept'red sway;
It is enthronèd in the hearts of kings,
It is an attribute to God himself,
195   And earthly power doth then show likest God's
When mercy seasons justice. Therefore, Jew,
Though justice be thy plea, consider this:
That, in the course of justice, none of us
Should see salvation.° We do pray for mercy,
200   And that same prayer doth teach us all to render
The deeds of mercy. I have spoke thus much
To mitigate the justice of thy plea;
Which if thou follow, this strict court of Venice
Must needs give sentence 'gainst the merchant there.

205   *Shylock.* My deeds upon my head! I crave the law,
The penalty and forfeit of my bond.

Portia. Is he not able to discharge the money?

Bassanio. Yes, here I tender it for him in the court,
Yea, twice° the sum. If that will not suffice,
210   I will be bound to pay it ten times o'er
On forfeit of my hands, my head, my heart.

---

183 **strained** constrained, compelled   198–99 **That . . . salvation**
(referring to the doctrine that God can justly condemn every man,
since none is free of sin)   209 **twice** (in lines 226 and 233 "thrice"
the money has been offered, and editors therefore commonly emend
"twice" to "thrice," on the assumption that here the compositor
misread the manuscript. But in line 84 the offered amount is indeed
double—six thousand ducats for three thousand—and therefore
emendation to "thrice" still leaves an inconsistency, unless the
point is that as Bassanio's fears for Antonio grow, he raises the
offer)

If this will not suffice, it must appear
That malice bears down truth. And I beseech you,
Wrest once the law to your authority.°
To do a great right, do a little wrong,   215
And curb this cruel devil of his will.

Portia. It must not be. There is no power in Venice
Can alter a decree establishèd.
'Twill be recorded for a precedent,
And many an error by the same example   220
Will rush into the state. It cannot be.

Shylock. A Daniel come to judgment!° Yea, a Daniel!
O wise young judge, how I do honor thee!

Portia. I pray you let me look upon the bond.

Shylock. Here 'tis, most reverend Doctor, here it is.   225

Portia. Shylock, there's thrice thy money off'red thee.

Shylock. An oath, an oath! I have an oath in heaven;
Shall I lay perjury upon my soul?
No, not for Venice!

Portia.   Why, this bond is forfeit;
And lawfully by this the Jew may claim   230
A pound of flesh, to be by him cut off
Nearest the merchant's heart. Be merciful.
Take thrice thy money; bid me tear the bond.

Shylock. When it is paid, according to the tenure.°
It doth appear you are a worthy judge;   235
You know the law, your exposition
Hath been most sound. I charge you by the law,
Whereof you are a well-deserving pillar,
Proceed to judgment. By my soul I swear
There is no power in the tongue of man   240
To alter me. I stay° here on my bond.

---

214 Wrest . . . authority for once twist the law a little and subject
it to your authority   222 A Daniel come to judgment the young
biblical hero who secured justice for Susanna (See Apocrypha,
Susannah: 42–64)   234 tenure conditions   241 stay take my stand

Antonio. Most heartily I do beseech the court
　　To give the judgment.

Portia.　　　　　　　　Why then, thus it is:
　　You must prepare your bosom for his knife—

245 *Shylock.* O noble judge! O excellent young man!

Portia. For the intent and purpose of the law
　　Hath full relation to° the penalty,
　　Which here appeareth due upon the bond.

Shylock. 'Tis very true. O wise and upright judge!
250　How much more elder art thou than thy looks!

Portia. Therefore lay bare your bosom.

Shylock.　　　　　　　　Ay, his breast—
　　So says the bond, doth it not, noble judge?
　　"Nearest his heart"; those are the very words.

Portia. It is so. Are there balance° here to weigh
　　The flesh?

255 *Shylock.*　　I have them ready.

Portia. Have by some surgeon, Shylock, on your
　　　　charge,°
　　To stop his wounds, lest he do bleed to death.

Shylock. Is it so nominated in the bond?

Portia. It is not so expressed, but what of that?
260　'Twere good you do so much for charity.

Shylock. I cannot find it; 'tis not in the bond.

Portia. You, merchant, have you anything to say?

Antonio. But little. I am armed and well prepared.
　　Give me your hand, Bassanio; fare you well.
265　Grieve not that I am fall'n to this for you,
　　For herein Fortune shows herself more kind
　　Than is her custom: it is still her use°

---

247 **Hath full relation to** is related inseparably to　254 **balance**
(plural) scales　256 **on your charge** at your expense　267 **still her
use** ever her custom

To let the wretched man outlive his wealth,
To view with hollow eye and wrinkled brow
An age of poverty; from which ling'ring penance   270
Of such misery doth she cut me off.
Commend me to your honorable wife.
Tell her the process° of Antonio's end,
Say how I loved you, speak me fair in death;
And when the tale is told, bid her be judge   275
Whether Bassanio had not once a love.°
Repent but you° that you shall lose your friend,
And he repents not° that he pays your debt;
For if the Jew do cut but deep enough,
I'll pay it instantly with all my heart.°   280

Bassanio. Antonio, I am married to a wife
Which is as dear to me as life itself;
But life itself, my wife, and all the world
Are not with me esteemed above thy life.
I would lose all, ay sacrifice them all   285
Here to this devil, to deliver you.

Portia. Your wife would give you little thanks for that
If she were by to hear you make the offer.

Gratiano. I have a wife who I protest I love.
I would she were in heaven, so she could   290
Entreat some power to change this currish Jew.

Nerissa. 'Tis well you offer it behind her back;
The wish would make else an unquiet house.

Shylock. These be the Christian husbands! I have a
    daughter;
Would any of the stock of Barabbas°   295
Had been her husband, rather than a Christian!
We trifle time. I pray thee pursue sentence.

---

273 **process** whole story   276 **love** friend (with a quibble on "love,"
in the sense of "lover")   277 **Repent but you** if you but feel sorrow
278 **And he repents not** then he regrets not   280 **with all my heart**
(a quibble on "heart" in the senses of soul and of the physical
organ)   295 **Barabbas** (1) the thief freed by Pilate when the people
demanded that Christ be crucified (2) the name of the villainous
hero in Marlowe's *The Jew of Malta*

Portia. A pound of that same merchant's flesh is thine.
The court awards it, and the law doth give it—

300 *Shylock.* Most rightful judge!

Portia. And you must cut this flesh from off his breast.
The law allows it, and the court awards it.

Shylock. Most learned judge! A sentence! Come, prepare!

Portia. Tarry a little; there is something else.
305 This bond doth give thee here no jot of blood;
The words expressly are "a pound of flesh."
Take then thy bond, take thou thy pound of flesh;
But in the cutting it, if thou dost shed
One drop of Christian blood, thy lands and goods
310 Are by the laws of Venice confiscate
Unto the state of Venice.

Gratiano. O upright judge! Mark, Jew. O learned
judge!

Shylock. Is that the law?

Portia.   Thyself shalt see the act;
For, as thou urgest justice, be assured
315 Thou shalt have justice more than thou desir'st.

Gratiano. O learned judge! Mark, Jew. A learned
judge!

Shylock. I take this offer then. Pay the bond thrice
And let the Christian go.

Bassanio.   Here is the money.

Portia. Soft!
320 The Jew shall have all justice. Soft, no haste;
He shall have nothing but the penalty.

Gratiano. O Jew! An upright judge, a learnèd judge!

Portia. Therefore prepare thee to cut off the flesh.
Shed thou no blood, nor cut thou less nor more
325 But just a pound of flesh. If thou tak'st more

Or less than a just° pound, be it but so much
As makes it light or heavy in the substance°
Or the division° of the twentieth part
Of one poor scruple°—nay, if the scale do turn
But in the estimation° of a hair—   330
Thou diest, and all thy goods are confiscate.

Gratiano. A second Daniel! A Daniel, Jew!
Now, infidel, I have you on the hip!

Portia. Why doth the Jew pause? Take thy forfeiture.

Shylock. Give me my principal, and let me go.   335

Bassanio. I have it ready for thee; here it is.

Portia. He hath refused it in the open court.
He shall have merely justice and his bond.

Gratiano. A Daniel still say I, a second Daniel!
I thank thee, Jew, for teaching me that word.   340

Shylock. Shall I not have barely my principal?

Portia. Thou shalt have nothing but the forfeiture,
To be so taken at thy peril, Jew.

Shylock. Why, then the devil give him good of it!
I'll stay no longer question.°

Portia.   Tarry, Jew!   345
The law hath yet another hold on you.
It is enacted in the laws of Venice,
If it be proved against an alien
That by direct or indirect attempts
He seek the life of any citizen,   350
The party 'gainst the which he doth contrive
Shall seize° one half his goods; the other half
Comes to the privy coffer° of the state;
And the offender's life lies in the mercy
Of the Duke only, 'gainst all other voice.   355

326 **just** exact 327 **substance** amount 328 **division** portion
328-29 **twentieth . . . scruple** i.e., one grain 330 **estimation** value
345 **stay no longer question** remain for no more talk 352 **seize**
take possession of 353 **privy coffer** equivalent to the British Privy
Purse, money provided for the monarch's own use

In which predicament° I say thou stand'st,
For it appears by manifest proceeding
That indirectly, and directly too,
Thou hast contrived against the very life
360 Of the defendant, and thou hast incurred
The danger formerly by me rehearsed.°
Down therefore, and beg mercy of the Duke.

Gratiano. Beg that thou mayst have leave to hang
  thyself!
And yet, thy wealth being forfeit to the state,
365 Thou hast not left the value of a cord;
Therefore thou must be hanged at the state's charge.

Duke. That thou shalt see the difference of our spirit,
I pardon thee thy life before thou ask it.
For° half thy wealth, it is Antonio's;
370 The other half comes to the general state,
Which humbleness may drive unto a fine.°

Portia. Ay, for the state, not for Antonio.

Shylock. Nay, take my life and all! Pardon not that!
You take my house, when you do take the prop
375 That doth sustain my house. You take my life
When you do take the means whereby I live.

Portia. What mercy can you render him, Antonio?

Gratiano. A halter gratis! Nothing else, for God's sake!

Antonio. So please my lord the Duke and all the court
380 To quit° the fine for one half of his goods,
I am content; so° he will let me have
The other half in use,° to render it
Upon his death unto the gentleman
That lately stole his daughter.
385 Two things provided more: that for this favor
He presently° become a Christian;
The other, that he do record a gift

---

356 **predicament** situation 361 **rehearsed** cited 369 **For** as for
371 **may drive unto a fine** may persuade me to reduce to a fine 380
quit remit 381 **so** provided 382 **in use** in trust, to use in his
business 386 **presently** instantly

Here in the court of all he dies possessed
Unto his son Lorenzo and his daughter.

Duke. He shall do this, or else I do recant°   390
The pardon that I late pronouncèd here.

Portia. Art thou contented, Jew? What dost thou say?

Shylock. I am content.

Portia.   Clerk, draw a deed of gift.

Shylock. I pray you give me leave to go from hence.
I am not well. Send the deed after me,   395
And I will sign it.

Duke.   Get thee gone, but do it.

Gratiano. In christ'ning shalt thou have two godfathers.
Had I been judge, thou shouldst have had ten
    more°—
To bring thee to the gallows, not to the font.

                                Exit [*Shylock*].

Duke. Sir, I entreat you home with me to dinner.   400

Portia. I humbly do desire your Grace of pardon.
I must away this night toward Padua,
And it is meet I presently set forth.

Duke. I am sorry that your leisure serves you not.°
Antonio, gratify° this gentleman,   405
For in my mind you are much bound to him.

                        Exit Duke and his Train.

Bassanio. Most worthy gentleman, I and my friend
Have by your wisdom been this day acquitted
Of grievous penalties, in lieu whereof,°
Three thousand ducats due unto the Jew   410
We freely cope° your courteous pains withal.

---

390 **recant** retract   398 **ten more** i.e., to make a jury of twelve
404 **serves you not** is not sufficient for you   405 **gratify** show your
gratitude to   409 **in lieu whereof** in return for   411 **We freely
cope** of our own free will we requite

Antonio. And stand indebted, over and above,
In love and service to you evermore.

415 *Portia.* He is well paid that is well satisfied,
And I, delivering you, am satisfied,
And therein do account myself well paid;
My mind was never yet more mercenary.
I pray you know me when we meet again.
I wish you well, and so I take my leave.

420 *Bassanio.* Dear sir, of force I must attempt you further.
Take some remembrance of us as a tribute,
Not as fee. Grant me two things, I pray you—
Not to deny me, and to pardon me.

Portia. You press me far, and therefore I will yield.
425 Give me your gloves; I'll wear them for your sake.
                    [*Bassanio takes off his gloves.*]
And for your love I'll take this ring from you.
Do not draw back your hand; I'll take no more,
And you in love° shall not deny me this.

Bassanio. This ring, good sir, alas, it is a trifle!
430 I will not shame myself to give you this.

Portia. I will have nothing else but only this,
And now methinks I have a mind to it.

Bassanio. There's more depends on this than on the
value.°
The dearest ring in Venice will I give you,
435 And find it out by proclamation.
Only for this, I pray you pardon me.°

Portia. I see, sir, you are liberal in offers.
You taught me first to beg, and now methinks
You teach me how a beggar should be answered.

440 *Bassanio.* Good sir, this ring was given me by my wife,
And when she put it on she made me vow
That I should neither sell nor give nor lose it.

428 in love in your good will to me   433 the value the ring's value
436 Only . . . pardon me only as for this ring, I beg you to excuse
me

Portia. That 'scuse serves many men to save their gifts.
　　And if your wife be not a madwoman,
　　And know how well I have deserved this ring,　　　*445*
　　She would not hold out enemy forever
　　For giving it to me. Well, peace be with you!
　　　　　　　　　　Exeunt [Portia and Nerissa].

Antonio. My Lord Bassanio, let him have the ring.
　　Let his deservings, and my love withal,
　　Be valued 'gainst your wife's commandement.°　　　*450*

Bassanio. Go, Gratiano, run and overtake him;
　　Give him the ring, and bring him if thou canst
　　Unto Antonio's house. Away, make haste!
　　　　　　　　　　　Exit Gratiano.
　　Come, you and I will thither presently,
　　And in the morning early will we both　　　*455*
　　Fly toward Belmont. Come, Antonio.　　　*Exeunt.*

[Scene II. *Venice. A street.*]

Enter [Portia and] Nerissa, [disguised as before].

Portia. Inquire the Jew's house out, give him this deed,°
　　And let him sign it. We'll away tonight
　　And be a day before our husbands home.
　　This deed will be well welcome to Lorenzo.

　　　　　　　　Enter Gratiano.

Gratiano. Fair sir, you are well o'erta'en.　　　*5*
　　My Lord Bassanio upon more advice°
　　Hath sent you here this ring, and doth entreat
　　Your company at dinner.

Portia.　　　　　　That cannot be.

450 **commandement** (four syllables)   IV.ii.1 **this deed** the deed of
gift for Lorenzo and Jessica   6 **upon more advice** on further consideration

His ring I do accept most thankfully,
10   And so I pray you tell him. Furthermore,
I pray you show my youth old Shylock's house.

Gratiano. That will I do.

Nerissa.   Sir, I would speak with you.
[*Aside to Portia*] I'll see if I can get my husband's
ring,
Which I did make him swear to keep forever.

Portia. [*Aside to Nerissa*] Thou mayst, I warrant. We
15   shall have old swearing°
That they did give the rings away to men;
But we'll outface them, and outswear them too.
Away, make haste! Thou know'st where I will tarry.

Nerissa. Come, good sir, will you show me to this
house?   [*Exeunt.*]

15 old swearing a lot of hard swearing

[ACT V

Scene I. *Belmont. A garden before Portia's house.*]

Enter Lorenzo and Jessica.

Lorenzo. The moon shines bright. In such a night as
    this,
When the sweet wind did gently kiss the trees
And they did make no noise, in such a night
Troilus° methinks mounted the Troyan walls,
And sighed his soul toward the Grecian tents   *5*
Where Cressid° lay that night.

Jessica.   In such a night
Did Thisbe° fearfully o'ertrip the dew,
And saw the lion's shadow ere himself,
And ran dismayed away.

Lorenzo.   In such a night
Stood Dido° with a willow° in her hand   *10*
Upon the wild sea banks, and waft° her love
To come again to Carthage.

V.i.1–23 (the lovers' playful contest in verse-making belongs to a type of poetic dialogue as old as Virgil's *Eclogues*)   4 **Troilus** hero of Chaucer's *Troilus and Cressida* and of Shakespeare's play of the same title; a type of the faithful lover   6 **Cressid** Cressida, a type of the faithless woman   7 **Thisbe** heroine of the tragic tale of *Pyramus and Thisbe* in Ovid's *Metamorphoses*   10 **Dido** Queen of Carthage whom Aeneas loved but abandoned at the call of duty   10 **willow** proverbially associated with forsaken love   11 **waft** waved (with the willow branch)

Jessica.   In such a night
    Medea° gathered the enchanted herbs
    That did renew old Aeson.°

Lorenzo.   In such a night
15   Did Jessica steal° from the wealthy Jew,
    And with an unthrift love° did run from Venice
    As far as Belmont.

Jessica.   In such a night
    Did young Lorenzo swear he loved her well,
    Stealing her soul with many vows of faith,
    And ne'er a true one.

20 *Lorenzo.*   In such a night
    Did pretty Jessica, like a little shrow,°
    Slander her love, and he forgave it her.

Jessica. I would out-night you, did nobody come;
    But hark, I hear the footing of a man.

Enter [Stephano,] a Messenger.

25 *Lorenzo.* Who comes so fast in silence of the night?

Messenger. A friend.

Lorenzo. A friend? What friend? Your name I pray
    you, friend.

Messenger. Stephano is my name, and I bring word
    My mistress will before the break of day
30   Be here at Belmont. She doth stray about
    By holy crosses° where she kneels and prays
    For happy wedlock hours.

Lorenzo.   Who comes with her?

Messenger. None but a holy hermit and her maid.
    I pray you, is my master yet returned?

13 **Medea** princess and sorceress who helped Jason to obtain the
Golden Fleece, and later was deserted by him   14 **Aeson** father of
Jason, restored to youth by Medea   15 **steal** (a pun) steal money,
steal away   16 **unthrift love** (a pun) a love which disregards wealth,
and a lover without wealth   21 **shrow** shrew   31 **holy crosses** (a
common sight in Renaissance Italy; used to mark shrines on hill-
tops, beside roads, etc.)

Lorenzo. He is not, nor we have not heard from him.   35
  But go we in, I pray thee, Jessica,
  And ceremoniously let us prepare
  Some welcome for the mistress of the house.

Enter [Launcelot, the] Clown.

Launcelot. Sola,° sola! Wo ha! Ho sola, sola!

Lorenzo. Who calls?   40

Launcelot. Sola! Did you see Master Lorenzo and
  Mistress Lorenzo? sola, sola!

Lorenzo. Leave holloaing, man! Here.

Launcelot. Sola! Where? Where?

Lorenzo. Here!   45

Launcelot. Tell him there's a post come from my
  master, with his horn full of good news.° My master
  will be here ere morning.   [*Exit.*]

Lorenzo. Sweet soul, let's in, and there expect° their
  coming.
  And yet no matter; why should we go in?   50
  My friend Stephano, signify, I pray you,
  Within the house, your mistress is at hand,
  And bring your music forth into the air.
                                      [*Exit Stephano.*]
  How sweet the moonlight sleeps upon this bank!   55
  Here will we sit and let the sounds of music
  Creep in our ears; soft stillness and the night
  Become° the touches° of sweet harmony.
  Sit, Jessica. Look how the floor of heaven
  Is thick inlaid with patens° of bright gold.
  There's not the smallest orb which thou behold'st   60
  But in his motion like an angel sings,

39 Sola (Launcelot imitates a courier's horn) 47 horn full of
good news (Launcelot puns on the cornucopia, "the horn of plenty")
49 expect await 57 Become befit 57, 67 touches notes produced
by touching the strings or stops of a musical instrument 59 patens
tiles

Still quiring° to the young-eyed cherubins;
Such harmony is in immortal souls,
But whilst this muddy vesture of decay°
63 Doth grossly close it in, we cannot hear it.

[*Enter Musicians.*]

Come ho, and wake Diana° with a hymn!
With sweetest touches pierce your mistress' ear
And draw her home with music.   *Play music.*

Jessica. I am never merry when I hear sweet music.

70 *Lorenzo.* The reason is, your spirits are attentive.
For do but note a wild and wanton° herd
Or race of youthful and unhandled colts
Fetching mad bounds, bellowing and neighing loud,
Which is the hot condition° of their blood:
75 If they but hear perchance a trumpet sound,
Or any air of music touch their ears,
You shall perceive them make a mutual stand,°
Their savage eyes turned to a modest gaze
By the sweet power of music. Therefore the poet
Did feign that Orpheus° drew trees, stones, and
80   floods;
Since naught so stockish,° hard, and full of rage°
But music for the time doth change his nature.
The man that hath no music in himself,
Nor is not moved with concord of sweet sounds,
85 Is fit for treasons, stratagems, and spoils;°
The motions° of his spirit are dull as night,
And his affections° dark as Erebus.°
Let no such man be trusted. Mark the music.

62 quiring making music (a reference to the music of the spheres.
It was thought that the harmonious movement of the spheres, in
Ptolemaic astronomy, produced a heavenly music inaudible to
human ears) 64 muddy vesture of decay earthy garment subject to
decay, i.e., the body 66 Diana goddess of the moon and of chastity
71 wanton frolicsome, untrained 74 hot condition impetuous na
ture 77 make a mutual stand stand still by common consent
80 Orpheus famous legendary Greek poet and musician 81 stockish
blockish, dull 81 rage passion 85 spoils plundering 86 motions
inward promptings 87 affections emotions 87 Erebus the dark
underworld of the Greeks

Enter Portia and Nerissa.

Portia. That light we see is burning in my hall;
   How far that little candle throws his beams!   *90*
   So shines a good deed in a naughty° world.

Nerissa. When the moon shone we did not see the
   candle.

Portia. So doth the greater glory dim the less.
   A substitute° shines brightly as a king
   Until a king be by, and then his state   *95*
   Empties itself,° as doth an inland brook
   Into the main of waters.° Music, hark!

Nerissa. It is your music, madam, of the house.

Portia. Nothing is good, I see, without respect;°
   Methinks it sounds much sweeter than by day.   *100*

Nerissa. Silence bestows that virtue on it, madam.

Portia. The crow doth sing as sweetly as the lark
   When neither is attended;° and I think
   The nightingale, if she should sing by day
   When every goose is cackling, would be thought   *105*
   No better a musician than the wren.
   How many things by season, seasoned are
   To their right praise and true perfection!°
   Peace! [*Music ceases.*] How the° moon sleeps with
     Endymion,°
   And would not be awaked.°

Lorenzo.   That is the voice,   *110*
   Or I am much deceived, of Portia.

---

91 **naughty** evil   94 **substitute** deputy   95–96 **his state/Empties itself**
i.e., his own glory merges into the king's   97 **main of waters** ocean
99 **without respect** without reference to circumstances   103 **attended**
heeded   107–08 **by season . . . perfection** by the right occasion are
made ready to receive their fitting praise and attain their full perfection   109 **Peace! How the** (the quarto reads "Peace, how the";
editors often emend to "Peace, ho! The")   109 **Endymion** a handsome shepherd, beloved of Diana   109–10 **Peace . . . awaked** addressed to the musicians

Portia. He knows me as the blind man knows the
    cuckoo,
    By the bad voice.

Lorenzo.   Dear lady, welcome home.

Portia. We have been praying for our husbands' welfare,
115   Which speed we hope the better for our words.
    Are they returned?

Lorenzo.   Madam, they are not yet,
    But there is come a messenger before
    To signify their coming.

Portia.   Go in, Nerissa.
    Give order to my servants that they take
120   No note at all of our being absent hence—
    Nor you, Lorenzo—Jessica, nor you.
                        [*A tucket° sounds.*]

Lorenzo. Your husband is at hand; I hear his trumpet.
    We are no telltales, madam; fear you not.

Portia. This night methinks is but the daylight sick;
125   It looks a little paler. 'Tis a day
    Such as the day is when the sun is hid.

Enter Bassanio, Antonio, Gratiano, and their Followers.

Bassanio. We should hold day with the Antipodes,°
    If you would walk in absence of the sun.

Portia. Let me give light,° but let me not be light,
130   For a light wife doth make a heavy° husband,
    And never be Bassanio so for me.
    But God sort all!° You are welcome home, my lord.

Bassanio. I thank you, madam. Give welcome to my
    friend.

121 s.d. **tucket** trumpet call (Bassanio, like every nobleman, had his
individual tucket)   127 **Antipodes** dwellers on the opposite side of
the earth   129, 130 **light, heavy** (Portia quibbles on "light" in the
senses of radiance, unchaste, and of little weight, and on "heavy" in
the senses of weighty and despondent, weighed down with trouble)
132 **God sort all** let God ordain all according to his wisdom

This is the man, this is Antonio,
To whom I am so infinitely bound.   135

Portia. You should in all sense° be much bound to him,
For, as I hear, he was much bound for you.

Antonio. No more than I am well acquitted of.°

Portia. Sir, you are very welcome to our house.
It must appear in other ways than words;   140
Therefore I scant this breathing courtesy.°

Gratiano. [*To Nerissa*] By yonder moon I swear you do
    me wrong!
In faith, I gave it to the judge's clerk.
Would he were gelt° that had it, for my part,°
Since you do take it, love, so much at heart.   145

Portia. A quarrel, ho, already! What's the matter?

Gratiano. About a hoop of gold, a paltry ring
That she did give me, whose posy° was
For all the world like cutler's poetry
Upon a knife, "Love me, and leave me not."   150

Nerissa. What° talk you of the posy or the value?
You swore to me when I did give it you
That you would wear it till your hour of death,
And that it should lie with you in your grave.
Though not for me,° yet for your vehement oaths,   155
You should have been respective° and have kept it.
Gave it a judge's clerk! No, God's my judge,
The clerk will ne'er wear hair on's face that had it!

Gratiano. He will, and if he live to be a man.

Nerissa. Ay, if a woman live to be a man.   160

Gratiano. Now by this hand, I gave it to a youth,
A kind of boy, a little scrubbèd° boy

---

136 **in all sense** (1) in all reason (2) in all senses   138 **acquitted of**
freed from   141 **breathing courtesy** courtesy that is only breath,
i.e., words   144 **gelt** castrated   144 **for my part** so far as I care
148 **posy** (a contraction of "poesy," i.e., "poetry") motto (inscribed
on a ring)   151 **What** why   155 **Though not for me** if not for my
sake   156 **respective** regardful, heedful   162 **scrubbèd** stunted

No higher than thyself, the judge's clerk,
A prating boy that begged it as a fee.
165   I could not for my heart deny it him.

Portia. You were to blame—I must be plain with you—
To part so slightly with your wife's first gift,
A thing stuck on with oaths upon your finger,
And so riveted with faith unto your flesh.
170   I gave my love a ring, and made him swear
Never to part with it; and here he stands.
I dare be sworn for him he would not leave it°
Nor pluck it from his finger, for the wealth
That the world masters.° Now in faith, Gratiano,
175   You give your wife too unkind° a cause of grief.
And, 'twere to me, I should be mad° at it.

Bassanio. [*Aside*] Why, I were best to cut my left hand
off
And swear I lost the ring defending it.

Gratiano. My Lord Bassanio gave his ring away
180   Unto the judge that begged it, and indeed
Deserved it too; and then the boy, his clerk
That took some pains in writing, he begged mine;
And neither man nor master would take aught
But the two rings.

Portia.   What ring gave you, my lord?
185   Not that, I hope, which you received of me.

Bassanio. If I could add a lie unto a fault,°
I would deny it; but you see my finger
Hath not the ring upon it—it is gone.

Portia. Even so void is your false heart of truth.
190   By heaven, I will ne'er come in your bed
Until I see the ring!

Nerissa.   Nor I in yours
Till I again see mine!

---

172 leave it let it go   174 masters possesses   175 unkind unnatur-
ally cruel   176 mad in a frenzy   186 fault faulty act

Bassanio.   Sweet Portia,
  If you did know to whom I gave the ring,
  If you did know for whom I gave the ring,
  And would conceive for what° I gave the ring,   195
  And how unwillingly I left the ring
  When naught would be accepted but the ring,
  You would abate the strength of your displeasure.

Portia. If you had known the virtue of the ring,
  Or half her worthiness that gave the ring,
  Or your own honor to contain° the ring,   200
  You would not then have parted with the ring.
  What man is there so much unreasonable,
  If you had pleased to have defended it
  With any terms of zeal,° wanted the modesty   205
  To urge the thing held as a ceremony?°
  Nerissa teaches me what to believe;
  I'll die for't but some woman had the ring!

Bassanio. No, by my honor, madam! By my soul
  No woman had it, but a civil doctor,°   210
  Which did refuse three thousand ducats of me
  And begged the ring, the which I did deny him,
  And suffered him to go displeased away,
  Even he that had held up the very life
  Of my dear friend. What should I say, sweet lady?   215
  I was enforced to send it after him.
  I was beset with shame and courtesy.°
  My honor would not let ingratitude
  So much besmear it. Pardon me, good lady!
  For by these blessèd candles of the night,   220
  Had you been there, I think you would have begged
  The ring of me to give the worthy doctor.

Portia. Let not that doctor e'er come near my house.

195 **conceive for what** form a conception of why   201 **honor to contain** honorable duty to retain   205 **terms of zeal** ardent language 205–06 **wanted . . . ceremony** would have been so lacking in modesty as to urge a claim on the thing you were keeping as a hallowed symbol   210 **civil doctor** doctor of civil law   217 **beset with shame and courtesy** assailed by feelings of shame and the obligations of courtesy

Since he hath got the jewel that I loved,
225 And that which you did swear to keep for me,
I will become as liberal° as you;
I'll not deny him anything I have,
No, not my body nor my husband's bed.
Know him I shall, I am well sure of it.
230 Lie not a night from home. Watch me like Argus.°
If you do not, if I be left alone—
Now by mine honor which is yet mine own,
I'll have that doctor for mine bedfellow.

Nerissa. And I his clerk. Therefore be well advised°
235 How you do leave me to mine own protection.

Gratiano. Well, do you so. Let not me take° him then!
For if I do, I'll mar the young clerk's pen.°

Antonio. I am th' unhappy subject of these quarrels.

Portia. Sir, grieve not you; you are welcome not with-
standing.

240 *Bassanio.* Portia, forgive me this enforcèd wrong,°
And in the hearing of these many friends
I swear to thee, even by thine own fair eyes,
Wherein I see myself—

Portia.   Mark you but that!
In both my eyes he doubly sees himself,
245 In each eye one. Swear by your double self,°
And there's an oath of credit.°

Bassanio.   Nay, but hear me.
Pardon this fault, and by my soul I swear
I never more will break an oath with thee.

Antonio. I once did lend my body for his wealth,°
250 Which but for him that had your husband's ring

---

226 **liberal** (1) licentious (2) generous   230 **Argus** a monstrous giant
of Greek myth, with a hundred eyes; a type of never-failing watch-
fulness   234 **be well advised** be very careful   236 **take** get hold of
237 **pen** (double entendre)   240 **this enforced wrong** this wrong I
was forced to commit   245 **double self** a quibble (1) twofold image
(2) double-dealing character   246 **oath of credit** oath to be believed
(spoken in irony)   249 **wealth** welfare

Had quite miscarried. I dare be bound again,
My soul upon the forfeit, that your lord
Will never more break faith advisedly.°

Portia. Then you shall be his surety. Give him this,
And bid him keep it better than the other.   *253*

Antonio. Here, Lord Bassanio. Swear to keep this ring.

Bassanio. By heaven, it is the same I gave the doctor!

Portia. I had it of him. Pardon me, Bassanio,
For by this ring the doctor lay with me.

Nerissa. And pardon me, my gentle Gratiano,   *260*
For that same scrubbèd boy, the doctor's clerk,
In lieu of° this, last night did lie with me.

Gratiano. Why, this is like the mending of highways
In summer, where the ways are fair enough.
What, are we cuckolds° ere we have deserved it?   *265*

Portia. Speak not so grossly. You are all amazed.°
Here is a letter; read it at your leisure.
It comes from Padua from Bellario.
There you shall find that Portia was the doctor,
Nerissa there her clerk. Lorenzo here   *270*
Shall witness I set forth as soon as you,
And even but now returned. I have not yet
Entered my house. Antonio, you are welcome,
And I have better news in store for you
Than you expect. Unseal this letter soon;   *275*
There you shall find three of your argosies
Are richly come to harbor suddenly.
You shall not know by what strange° accident
I chancèd on this letter.

Antonio.   I am dumb!

Bassanio. Were you the doctor, and I knew you not?   *280*

---

253 **advisedly** deliberately   262 **In lieu of** in return for   265 **cuckolds** husbands of faithless wives   266 **amazed** utterly bewildered; literally, entangled in a maze or labyrinth   278 **strange** astonishing

Gratiano. Were you the clerk that is to make me
cuckold?

Nerissa. Ay, but the clerk that never means to do it,
Unless he live until he be a man.

Bassanio. Sweet Doctor, you shall be my bedfellow.
285   When I am absent, then lie with my wife.

Antonio. Sweet lady, you have given me life and living!
For here I read for certain that my ships
Are safely come to road.°

Portia.   How now, Lorenzo?
My clerk hath some good comforts too for you.

290   *Nerissa.* Ay, and I'll give them him without a fee.
There do I give to you and Jessica
From the rich Jew, a special deed of gift,
After his death, of all he dies possessed of.

Lorenzo. Fair ladies, you drop manna in the way
Of starvèd people.°

295   *Portia.*   It is almost morning,
And yet I am sure you are not satisfied
Of these events at full.° Let us go in,
And charge us there upon° inter'gatories,°
And we will answer all things faithfully.

300   *Gratiano.* Let it be so. The first inter'gatory
That my Nerissa shall be sworn on° is,
Whether till the next night she had rather stay,
Or go to bed now, being two hours to day.
But were the day come, I should wish it dark
305   Till I were couching with the doctor's clerk.
Well, while I live I'll fear no other thing
So sore, as keeping safe Nerissa's ring.   *Exeunt.*

FINIS

288 road anchorage   **295 starvèd people** (Lorenzo, though of good
social position, was, like Bassanio, far from rich)   **296–97 not satisfied . . . full** not fully satisfied how these events came to pass   **298
charge us there upon** load us with questions   **298 inter'gatories**
interrogatories, i.e., questions formally drawn up to be put to a
defendant or witness and answered under oath   **301 sworn on**
sworn to under oath

Textual Note

The exact date of the play's composition is uncertain, but the play was in existence in 1598, when Francis Meres mentioned it in *Palladis Tamia,* and it may have been written as early as 1596, if the reference to the ship *Andrew* in I.i.27 is indebted—as has been conjectured—to news of the capture of the Spanish ship *St. Andrew* in the Cádiz expedition. In 1598 and in 1600 the play was entered in the Stationers' Register. It was first published in a quarto (Q1) in 1600. The interesting part of the title page runs thus: "The most excellent/ Historie of the Merchant/ of Venice./ With the extreame crueltie of Shylocke the Iewe/ towards the sayd Merchant, in cutting a iust pound/ of his flesh: and the obtayning of Portia/ by the choyse of three/ chests./ As it hath beene diuers times acted by the Lord/ Chamberlaine his Seruants./ Written by William Shakespeare." The absence of some necessary stage directions (e.g., entrances of some characters who later speak) suggests that the copy for this quarto could not have been a promptbook. Conversely, there are some bits of evidence that suggest the copy was very close to Shakespeare's manuscript; for example, such a stage direction as "Enter Portia for Balthazar" seems to reflect an author's conception of his action. But plays that are commonly thought to be printed from Shakespeare's manuscript usually have some confusions in them, the result of a somewhat illegible manuscript, and *The Merchant* lacks such confusions. Probably, then, the printer's copy for the first quarto was a scribe's careful and clean copy of the manuscript—but, of course, it is unwise to be dogmatic about such matters.

In 1619 a second quarto (Q2) appeared, falsely dated 1600. Q2 was based on Q1, and though it corrects some palpable errors in Q1, Q2 has no independent authority. In 1623 the play was again reprinted, in the First Folio, again from Q1. And again, of course, there are some slight departures from Q1, ranging from misprints to the addition of some interesting stage directions that doubtless reflect playhouse practice. The most notable are directions calling for the flourishing of cornets.

Q1, then, the only authoritative text, and the source of all others, serves as the basis for the present edition, but some changes have been made. Solanio, Salarino, and Salerio have, as in most modern editions, been reduced to Solanio and Salerio. (Possibly Shakespeare began with three such characters in mind, but as he worked he apparently found he could make do with two, and Salarino disappeared. The name Salarino—which in Q1 occurs in stage directions at I.i; II.iv, vi, viii; III.i—in this edition is replaced by Salerio. Salarino is a diminutive of Salerio, and it is possible that Shakespeare did not intend them to be distinct. In any case, the name Salerio must stay, because it appears in the dialogue as well as in the stage directions.) Spelling and punctuation have been modernized, and speech prefixes have been regularized (e.g., we give "Shylock," though Q1 varies between "Shylock," "Shy.," and "Iew"). Act divisions, first introduced in the Folio, are given, and for ease of reference, the scene divisions established by the Globe edition are given. These additions, like necessary stage directions that are not found in Q1, are enclosed in square brackets. A superfluous stage direction ("*Enter Tubal*," at III.i.74) has been deleted, the positions of a few stage directions are slightly altered, and obvious typographical errors have been corrected. Other departures from Q1 are listed below, the adopted reading given first, in *italic* type, the rejected reading in roman type. If the adopted reading comes from Q2 or F, that fact is indicated.

I.i.27 *docked* docks   113 *Is* It is

I.ii.59 *throstle* Trassell

II.i.s.d. *Morocco* Morochus   35 *page* rage

II.ii.99 *last* [Q2] lost

II.vii.69 *tombs* timber

II.viii.39 *Slubber* [Q2, F] slumber

III.i.100 *Heard* heere

III.ii.67 eyes [F] eye   81 *vice* voyce

III.iii.s.d. *Solanio* Salerio

III.iv.49 *Padua* Mantua   50 *cousin's* [Q2, F] cosin   81 *my* [Q2, F] my my

III.v.21 *e'en* [Q2, F] in   27 *comes.* come?   77 *merit it* meane it, it   84 *a wife* [F] wife

IV.i.30 *his state* [Q2, F] this states   31 *flint* [Q2] flints   51 *Master* Maisters   74 *bleat* [F] bleake   75 *mountain* [F] mountaine of   100 *is mine* as mine   229 *No, not* [Q2] Not not   396 *Gratiano* [Q2, F] Shy [lock]

V.i.41–42 *Master Lorenzo and Mistress Lorenzo?* M. Lorenzo, & M. Lorenzo   49 *Sweet soul* [concludes Launcelot's speech]   51 *Stephano* [Q2] Stephen   87 *Erebus* [F] Terebus   152 *it you* [Q2, F] you

The Merchant of Venice

Some of Shakespeare's plays are close to their sources, and it is useful and often illuminating to see how he departs from Plutarch or Holinshed, Greene or Lodge. But no known work can be the only source for *The Merchant of Venice.* Apparently Shakespeare combined a number of sources, all of which repay careful study.

If he drew chiefly on a single source, it may have been a play called *The Jew,* which Stephen Gosson mentioned favorably in 1579, in his *School of Abuse,* and which he said showed "the greediness of worldly choosers" and the "bloody minds of usurers." Some scholars believe that the term "worldly choosers" shows that the casket story (in which worldly-minded suitors are discomfited by choosing the gold or silver casket) has been combined with the story of the usurer and the pound of flesh. Yet the word "greediness" seems less appropriate to suitors than to usurers. In any case, *The Jew* is not extant, and speculation about Shakespeare's debt to it is idle.

Of extant works, *Il Pecorone* (The Dunce), an Italian collection of prose tales by an author who calls himself Ser Giovanni Fiorentino, is the most relevant. The first tale of the fourth day concerns the Lady of Belmonte, a widow who demands that each traveler seek to possess her; if he does, she will wed him, but if he fails, all his goods are forfeit. Giannetto voyages to Belmonte twice; twice he is drugged and therefore fails and loses his goods. His godfather then borrows from a Jewish usurer and furnishes him for a third voyage. (Giannetto has lied, telling his godfather that the goods were lost in shipwrecks.) This time Giannetto—warned by the Lady's maid—is successful. There follows the usurer's demand for the overdue money, the cleverness of the lawyer, the Lady in disguise (as in Shakespeare), and the business of the ring.

There is no indubitable proof that Shakespeare borrowed directly from *Il Pecorone.* He could have found the tale of the pound of flesh in other works, such as Alexander Silvayne's *The Orator* and Anthony Munday's *Zelauto.* It seems more than possible, however, that Shakespeare read *Il Pecorone* either in a translation or in Italian—a language which, with his good knowledge of Latin, he might very easily have acquired.

If he read it in one language or another, probably his most notable changes are the alteration of the indecent test imposed on the wooer, the addition of the usurer's daughter, and the omission of the wooer's incredibly long forgetfulness of his benefactor's danger, together with the ennoblement of all the leading characters.

The story of the caskets comes ultimately from Oriental folklore. Shakespeare's immediate source is believed to be an English version of the *Gesta Romanorum,* a collection of medieval Latin tales, translated into English in 1577 and "bettered" by the same translator in 1595. Possibly the author of the old play *The Jew* is responsible for joining the casket plot to the bond plot, but we know little about that play; Shakespeare may have been the first to combine the two stories.

Finally, it should be mentioned that Shakespeare's play about Christians and a Jew must owe something to Marlowe's *The Jew of Malta,* and also to the trial, in 1594, of Dr. Roderigo Lopez, the converted Portuguese Jew who, though very probably innocent, was convicted and executed on the charge of plotting to poison Queen Elizabeth I. In *The Jew of Malta,* Shakespeare would have found a Jew who is a scoundrel but is, at certain moments, a really human figure wronged by the Christians around him. Shylock's daughter Jessica may owe something to Marlowe's Abigail, who loves a Christian, but both Abigail and her beloved are killed, whereas Jessica escapes into a happy marriage with Lorenzo. In the Lopez trial, Shakespeare would have found the usual depiction of the murderous Jew.

Geoffrey Bullough, in the first volume of his *Narrative and Dramatic Sources of Shakespeare,* has brought together selections from Silvayne's *The Orator,* Anthony Munday's *Zelauto,* and *Il Pecorone.* To anyone who browses through this material, it is clear enough that Shakespeare did not invent the chief episodes of his play. It is no less clear that the remarkable characterizations, the moral tone, the poetry, and probably the deft interweaving of the various strands of the plot are the work of a great dramatic poet.

Commentaries

NICHOLAS ROWE

from *The Works of Mr. William Shakespear*

In *Twelfth Night* there is something singularly ridiculous and pleasant in the fantastical steward Malvolio. . . . Petruchio, in *The Taming of the Shrew,* is an uncommon piece of humor. . . . To these I might add that incomparable character of Shylock the Jew, in *The Merchant of Venice;* but though we have seen that play received and acted as a comedy, and the part of the Jew performed by an excellent comedian, yet I cannot but think it was designed tragically by the author. There appears in it such a deadly spirit of revenge, such a savage fierceness and fellness, and such a bloody designation of cruelty and mischief, as cannot agree either with the style or characters of comedy. The play itself, take it all together, seems to me to be one of the most finished of any of Shakespear's. The tale, indeed, in that part relating to the caskets, and the extravagant and unusual kind of bond given by Antonio, is a little too much removed from the rules of probability: but taking the fact for granted, we must allow it to be very beautifully written. There is something in the friendship of Antonio to Bassanio very great, generous, and tender. The whole fourth act, supposing, as I said, the fact to be probable, is extremely fine. But there are two passages that deserve a particular notice. The first is what Portia says in praise of mercy, and the other on the power of music. [1709]

WILLIAM HAZLITT

from *Characters of Shakespear's Plays*

This is a play that in spite of the change of manners and prejudices still holds undisputed possession of the stage. Shakespear's malignant has outlived Mr. Cumberland's benevolent Jew. In proportion as Shylock has ceased to be a popular bugbear, "baited with the rabble's curse," he becomes a half-favorite with the philosophical part of the audience, who are disposed to think that Jewish revenge is at least as good as Christian injuries. Shylock is *a good hater;* "a man no less sinned against than sinning." If he carries his revenge too far, yet he has strong grounds for "the lodged hate he bears Anthonio," which he explains with equal force of eloquence and reason. He seems the depositary of the vengeance of his race; and though the long habit of brooding over daily insults and injuries has crusted over his temper with inveterate misanthropy, and hardened him against the contempt of mankind, this adds but little to the triumphant pretensions of his enemies. There is a strong, quick, and deep sense of justice mixed up with the gall and bitterness of his resentment. The constant apprehension of being burnt alive, plundered, banished, reviled, and trampled on, might be supposed to sour the most forbearing nature, and to take something from that "milk of human kindness," with which his persecutors contemplated his indignities. The desire of revenge is almost inseparable from the sense of wrong; and we can hardly help sympathizing with the proud spirit, hid beneath his "Jewish gaberdine,"

From *Characters of Shakespear's Plays* by William Hazlitt. 2nd ed. London: Taylor & Hessey, 1818.

stung to madness by repeated undeserved provocations, and laboring to throw off the load of obloquy and oppression heaped upon him and all his tribe by one desperate act of "lawful" revenge, till the ferociousness of the means by which he is to execute his purpose, and the pertinacity with which he adheres to it, turn us against him; but even at last, when disappointed of the sanguinary revenge with which he had glutted his hopes, and exposed to beggary and contempt by the letter of the law on which he had insisted with so little remorse, we pity him, and think him hardly dealt with by his judges. In all his answers and retorts upon his adversaries, he has the best not only of the argument but of the question, reasoning on their own principles and practice. They are so far from allowing of any measure of equal dealing, of common justice or humanity between themselves and the Jew, that even when they come to ask a favor of him, and Shylock reminds them that "on such a day they spit upon him, another spurned him, another called him dog, and for these curtesies request he'll lend them so much monies"—Anthonio, his old enemy, instead of any acknowledgment of the shrewdness and justice of his remonstrance, which would have been preposterous in a respectable Catholic merchant in those times, threatens him with a repetition of the same treatment—

> "I am as like to call thee so again,
> To spit on thee again, to spurn thee too."

After this, the appeal to the Jew's mercy, as if there were any common principle of right and wrong between them, is the rankest hypocrisy, or the blindest prejudice; and the Jew's answer to one of Anthonio's friends, who asks him what his pound of forfeit flesh is good for, is irresistible—

> "To bait fish withal; if it will feed nothing else, it will feed my revenge. He hath disgrac'd me, and hinder'd me of half a million, laughed at my losses, mock'd at my gains, scorn'd my nation, thwarted my bargains, cool'd my friends, heated mine enemies; and what's his reason? I am a Jew. Hath not a Jew eyes; hath not a Jew hands, organs, dimensions,

senses, affections, passions; fed with the same food, hurt with the same weapons, subject to the same diseases, healed by the same means, warmed and cooled by the same winter and summer that a Christian is? If you prick us, do we not bleed? If you tickle us, do we not laugh? If you poison us, do we not die? And if you wrong us, shall we not revenge? If we are like you in the rest, we will resemble you in that. If a Jew wrong a Christian, what is his humility? revenge. If a Christian wrong a Jew, what should his sufferance be by Christian example? why revenge. The villainy you teach me I will execute, and it shall go hard but I will better the instruction."

The whole of the trial scene, both before and after the entrance of Portia, is a masterpiece of dramatic skill. The legal acuteness, the passionate declamations, the sound maxims of jurisprudence, the wit and irony interspersed in it, the fluctuations of hope and fear in the different persons, and the completeness and suddenness of the catastrophe, cannot be surpassed. Shylock, who is his own counsel, defends himself well, and is triumphant on all the general topics that are urged against him, and only fails through a legal flaw. Take the following as an instance—

"*Shylock.* What judgment shall I dread, doing no wrong?
You have among you many a purchas'd slave,
Which like your asses, and your dogs, and mules,
You use in abject and in slavish part,
Because you bought them:—shall I say to you,
Let them be free, marry them to your heirs?
Why sweat they under burdens? let their beds
Be made as soft as yours, and let their palates
Be season'd with such viands? you will answer,
The slaves are ours:—so do I answer you:
The pound of flesh, which I demand of him,
Is dearly bought, is mine, and I will have it:
If you deny me, fie upon your law!
There is no force in the decrees of Venice:
I stand for judgment: answer; shall I have it?"

The keenness of his revenge awakes all his faculties; and

he beats back all opposition to his purpose, whether grave or gay, whether of wit or argument, with an equal degree of earnestness and self-possession. His character is displayed as distinctly in other less prominent parts of the play, and we may collect from a few sentences the history of his life —his descent and origin, his thrift and domestic economy, his affection for his daughter, whom he loves next to his wealth, his courtship and his first present to Leah, his wife! "I would not have parted with it" (the ring which he first gave her) "for a wilderness of monkies!" What a fine Hebraism is implied in this expression!

Portia is not a very great favorite with us; neither are we in love with her maid, Nerissa. Portia has a certain degree of affectation and pedantry about her, which is very unusual in Shakespear's women, but which perhaps was a proper qualification for the office of a "civil doctor," which she undertakes and executes so successfully. The speech about Mercy is very well; but there are a thousand finer ones in Shakespeare. We do not admire the scene of the caskets: and object entirely to the Black Prince, Morocchius. We should like Jessica better if she had not deceived and robbed her father, and Lorenzo, if he had not married a Jewess, though he thinks he has a right to wrong a Jew. The dialogue between this newly-married couple by moonlight, beginning "On such a night," etc., is a collection of classical elegancies. Launcelot, the Jew's man, is an honest fellow. The dilemma in which he describes himself placed between his "conscience and the fiend," the one of which advises him to run away from his master's service and the other to stay in it, is exquisitely humorous.

Gratiano is a very admirable subordinate character. He is the jester of the piece: yet one speech of his, in his own defense, contains a whole volume of wisdom.

"*Anthonio.* I hold the world but as the world, Gratiano,
A stage, where every one must play his part;
And mine a sad one.
Gratiano. Let me play the fool:
With mirth and laughter let old wrinkles come;
And let my liver rather heat with wine,

Than my heart cool with mortifying groans.
Why should a man, whose blood is warm within,
Sit like his grandsire cut in alabaster?
Sleep when he wakes? and creep into the jaundice
By being peevish? I tell thee what, Anthonio—
I love thee, and it is my love that speaks;—
There are a sort of men, whose visages
Do cream and mantle like a standing pond:
And do a wilful stillness entertain,
With purpose to be drest in an opinion
Of wisdom, gravity, profound conceit;
As who should say, *I am Sir Oracle,*
And when I ope my lips, let no dog bark!
O, my Anthonio, I do know of these,
That therefore only are reputed wise,
For saying nothing; who, I am very sure,
If they should speak, would almost damn those ears,
Which hearing them, would call their brothers, fools.
I'll tell thee more of this another time:
But fish not with this melancholy bait,
For this fool's gudgeon, this opinion."

Gratiano's speech on the philosophy of love, and the effect of habit in taking off the force of passion, is as full of spirit and good sense. The graceful winding up of this play in the fifth act, after the tragic business is despatched, is one of the happiest instances of Shakespear's knowledge of the principles of the drama. We do not mean the pretended quarrel between Portia and Nerissa and their husbands about the rings, which is amusing enough, but the conversation just before and after the return of Portia to her own house, beginning "How sweet the moonlights sleeps upon this bank," and ending "Peace! how the moon sleeps with Endymion, and would not be awaked." There is a number of beautiful thoughts crowded into that short space, and linked together by the most natural transitions.

When we first went to see Mr. Kean in Shylock, we expected to see, what we had been used to see, a decrepit old man, bent with age and ugly with mental deformity, grinning with deadly malice, with the venom of his heart congealed in the expression of his countenance, sullen, morose, gloomy, inflexible, brooding over one idea, that of his hatred, and fixed on one unalterable purpose, that of his revenge. We were disappointed, because we had taken our idea from other actors, not from the play. There is no proof there that Shylock is old, but a single line, "Bassanio and *old* Shylock, both stand forth"—which does not imply that he is infirm with age—and the circumstance that he has a daughter marriageable, which does not imply that he is old at all. It would be too much to say that his body should be made crooked and deformed to answer to his mind, which is bowed down and warped with prejudices and passion. That he has but one idea is not true; he has more ideas than any other person in the piece; and if he is intense and inveterate in the pursuit of his purpose, he shows the utmost elasticity, vigor, and presence of mind, in the means of attaining it. But so rooted was our habitual impression of the part from seeing it caricatured in the representation, that it was only from a careful perusal of the play itself that we saw our error. The stage is not in general the best place to study our author's characters in. It is too often filled with traditional commonplace conceptions of the part, handed down from sire to son, and suited to the taste of *the great vulgar and the small*—" 'Tis an unweeded garden: things rank and gross do merely gender in it!" If a man of genius comes once in an age to clear away the rubbish, to make it fruitful and wholesome, they cry, " 'Tis a bad school: it may be like nature, it may be like Shakespear, but it is not like us." Admirable critics!

ANONYMOUS

Henry Irving's Shylock

The production by Mr. Irving at the Lyceum of *The Merchant of Venice* was eagerly expected and had a double source of certain attraction. The beauties of Miss Ellen Terry's Portia were already known; those of Mr. Irving's Shylock had to be discovered. The character of Shylock has given food for much discussion. It is well known that modern interpretations of the part have differed entirely from those given by the actors who, before the days of Macklin, treated the part from the point of view of the most grotesque comedy; and a good many people have told us how Shakspeare intended it to be treated. Mr. Hawkins, in the current number of the *Theatre* magazine, has argued very ingeniously and interestingly, from the fact that *The Merchant of Venice* appeared during the excitement caused by the iniquities of the Jew physician, Rodrigo Lopez, that the play was intended by its author as "a plea for toleration towards the Jews." The theory is well worked out and hangs well enough together, since it is admitted that, supposing this to have been Shakspeare's intention, his position as a manager, bound to please his public, hampered him in its execution. But we have always been of opinion that theorizing as to Shakspeare's intentions and the meanings of his characters, however interesting it may be as an exercise of ingenuity, has little practical import. It will hardly seem probable that Shakspeare was in the habit of sitting down with a set purpose to teach certain moral lessons by means of certain characters, to be rendered in certain definite ways; and yet one might infer from the work of commentators that this was the case. No manager or play-writer could believe that any part would ever be given in precisely the same way by any two actors, except so far as it might be done by servile imitation; and, indeed, to make this possible would involve a degradation of character to caricature. Such a broad rule as that Shylock ought not to be played as a low-comedy part, or that Lear ought not to be from beginning to end a driveling idiot, may of course be laid down; but one has surely no more right to expect an actor to execute a part in the way imagined to be right by commentators than to demand that a painter should seize just this or that aspect of a great historical subject. The enthusiasm aroused by Mr. Irving's Shylock, even in those who find his rendering of the character differ from their view of it, goes, however, to prove that, as has been suggested, an elaborate analysis of Shakspeare's characters made from studying the text is valuable chiefly as a mental exercise.

Mr. Irving presents Shylock as a picturesque figure, with an air as of a man feeling the bitterness of oppression, and conscious of his own superiority in all but circumstance to the oppressor—a feeling which is finely indicated when, in talk with Antonio, he touches the Christian merchant, and, seeing the action resented, bows deprecatingly, with an af-fectation of deep humility. He dwells with concentrated bitterness on the expressions of hatred to Antonio in the speech beginning "How like a fawning publican he looks;" and here, in the implacable determination of "If I can catch him once upon the hip, I will feed fat the ancient grudge I bear him," we have the prologue, as it were, to the intense revengefulness of the last scene. It may be noted that since the first night Mr. Irving's performance has gained in leading up consistently to its climax—as consistently, that is, as is possible in the case of a human creature worked on by mixed emotions which sometimes baffle scrutiny. The point which on the first night seemed most striking to many people in the general scope of the actor's representation was that his Shylock was intended to be, before all things, digni-fied, and it was thought that his acting in the scene when he bewails the loss of his daughter and his ducats was at variance with the rest of the performance. It would perhaps be neither easy nor desirable to make Shylock altogether dignified at this point; but it is not the less true that Mr. Irving has improved the rendering of this scene, and, with it, the whole value of his representation.

To return, however, to Mr. Irving's first scene, we may note specially the bitterness of subdued scorn in the speech beginning "Signior Antonio, many a time and oft in the Rialto you have rated me," and the diabolical mockery of good humor with which he proposes the "merry bond." In the next scene in which the Jew appears we have again his hatred and desire for revenge marked strongly in the resolution to go forth to supper "in hate, to feed upon the prodigal Christian," and to part with Launcelot "to one that I would have him help to waste his borrowed purse;" and at the end of the act Mr. Irving has introduced a singularly fine touch of invention. Lorenzo has fled with his stolen bride and her stolen money, and a crowd of masquers has crossed the stage and disappeared over the picturesque bridge with laughter and music. Then Shylock is seen, lantern in hand, advancing, bent in thought; and, as he comes close to his robbed and deserted house, the curtain falls. The effect, however, would, to our thinking, be doubled if the curtain had not fallen for a moment and been raised again just before this appearance of Shylock—if the masquers had disappeared in sight of the audience, and the sounds of revelry had died away in the distance. It may be conjectured that the dropping of the curtain signifies the interval of time which might naturally elapse between the elopement and Shylock's return; but this is, we think, needless. Mr. Irving, in the scene already referred to of the third act, is now less vehement than might have been expected; the Jew's passion seems to have exhausted him, but is not for that the less intense in itself. He is overweighted with trouble, and the delivery of the words "no ill luck stirring, but what lights o' my shoulders; no sighs, but o' my breathing; no tears, but o' my shedding," is charged with the pathos of the heaviest grief, and it may be the importance given by the actor's feeling and art to this passage which makes one

think that less than its due value is given to the following
passage about Leah's ring.

It is, however, in the fourth act, as is fitting, that the
actor's complete triumph is attained, and in this there seems
to us no room for anything but admiration. From the moment of his entrance to that of his finding his revenge torn
from him he is the very incarnation of deadly, resistless
hatred. While he listens to the Duke's speech in mitigation
he has the horrible stillness and fascination of the rattle-
snake. When he answers, his speech is that of a man possessed of his purpose, coldly tenacious of his rights. His
object has been gained, and the passion which has been
concentrated on it will not deign to waste itself in support-
ing a position that is unassailable. His scorn of Gratiano's
railings seems bitter from habit, and not because he is one
whit moved by them. There is something appalling in his
aspect when he stands waiting for the long desired moment
with the knife in one hand and the scales in the other, and
his pointing to the bond with the knife as he asks, "Is it so
nominated in the bond?" is admirably conceived and executed. When the moment of defeat arrives it strikes him
like lightning, but its effect, like that of his expected triumph, is so powerful that it cannot find expression in any
accustomed use of gesture or attitude. He is still in his despair as in his victory; but it is the stillness of one suffering
instead of threatening death. Where he before inspired terror, he cannot now but command respect for the very awful-
ness of his downthrow. He leaves the court with a dignity
that seems the true expression of his belief in his nation and
himself. His mind is occupied with greater matters than the
light jeers of Gratiano, and to these jeers he replies with
three slow downward movements of the head, which are infinitely expressive of his acceptance of that which has be-
fallen him and of his power to bear himself nobly under its
weight. "Gratiano speaks an infinite deal of nothing," and
what he says at this moment seems empty indeed when
answered with this silent eloquence. Nothing could be finer
than Mr. Irving's acting at this point, which is the climax
of a scene the power and imagination of which can scarcely
be rivaled.

The striking excellences of Miss Ellen Terry's Portia are, if anything, bettered by being transferred to a larger stage than that on which they were first presented to a London audience. Every changing phase of the part is rendered with the highest instinct and art, and every change seems natural and easy. The tenderness; the love so fine that it finds no check to open acknowledgment; the wit, the dignity; and in the last scene the desire to be merciful and to inspire mercy, giving way to a just and overwhelming wrath, and followed again by the natural playfulness of the lady who is not the less a great lady because she indulges it, are alike rendered with a skill that one must call perfect. As feats of acting the assumption to Nerissa of a bragging youth's manner, and the exit in the trial scene are specially remarkable; but it is needless to point out in detail the patent beauties of a performance with which we can find no fault.

ELMER EDGAR STOLL

from *Shylock*

As much as fifteen years ago[1] Professor Wendell expressed the opinion, which Professor Matthews has of late reasserted, that Shylock was rightly represented on the stage in Shakespeare's time as a comic character, and rightly in our time as sympathetically human; but the dramatist's intention he left in the dark. . . .

The dramatist's intention—that, I must believe, together with his success or failure in fulfilling it, is the only matter of importance. . . .

Only now and then have critics frankly denied it, and declared that the purpose of the author has only an historical interest. That way, they seem to see, if not madness, chaos lies. For thus a work of art means anything, everything—that is, nothing—and what is the use of discussing it? . . .

The puzzle whether *The Merchant of Venice* is not meant for tragedy . . . is cleared up when, as Professor Baker suggests, we forget Sir Henry Irving's acting, and remember that the title—and the hero—is not the "Jew of Venice" as he would lead us to suppose. . . .

Hero or not, Shylock is given a villain's due. His is the heaviest penalty to be found in all the pound of flesh

From *Shakespeare Studies* by E. E. Stoll. New York: The Macmillan Company, 1927. Grateful acknowledgment is made to Mrs. Doris Franklin for permission to reprint these excerpts.

[1] This essay was written in 1911. The editor has abbreviated it and deleted the footnotes citing abundant authorities. The remaining footnotes have been renumbered [editor's note].

stories, including that in *Il Pecorone*, which served as a model for the play . . . —impoverishment, sentence of death, and an outrage done to his faith from which Jews were guarded even by decrees of German emperors and Roman pontiffs. . . . We know that the poet is not with Shylock, for on that point, in this play as in every other, the impartial, inscrutable poet leaves little or nothing to suggestion or surmise. As is his custom elsewhere, by the comments of the good characters, by the methods pursued in the disposition of scenes, and by the downright avowals of soliloquy, he constantly sets us right.

As for the first of these artifices, all the people who come in contact with Shylock except Tubal—among them being those of his own house, his servant and his daughter—have a word or two to say on the subject of his character, and never a good one. And in the same breath they spend on Bassanio and Antonio, his enemies, nothing but words of praise. . . .

As for the second artifice, the ordering of the scenes is such as to enforce this contrast. . . . Launcelot and Jessica, in separate scenes, are introduced before Shylock reaches home, that, hearing their story, we may side with them, and, when the old curmudgeon appears, may be moved to laughter as he complains of Launcelot's gormandizing, sleeping, and rending apparel out. . . . Still more conspicuous is this care when Shylock laments over his daughter and his ducats. Lest then by any chance a stupid or tender-hearted audience should not laugh but grieve, Solanio reports his outcries—in part word for word—two scenes in advance, as matter of mirth to himself and all the boys in Venice. . . .

As for the third artifice, that a sleepy audience may not make the mistake of the cautious critic and take the villain for the hero, Shakespeare is at pains to label the villain by an aside at the moment the hero appears on the boards:

> I hate him for he is a Christian,
> But more for that in low simplicity
> He lends out money gratis, and brings down
> The rate of usance here with us in Venice.

Those are his motives, later confessed repeatedly;[2] and either one brands him a villain more unmistakably in that day, as we shall see, than in ours. . . .

Only twice does Shakespeare seem to follow Shylock's pleadings and reasonings with any sympathy—"Hath a dog money?" in the first scene in which he appears, and "Hath not a Jew eyes"? in the third act—but a bit too much has been made of this. Either plea ends in such fashion as to alienate the audience. To Shylock's reproaches the admirable Antonio, "one of the gentlest and humblest of all the men in Shakespeare's theater" [i.e., dramas], praised and honored by everyone but Shylock, retorts, secure in his virtue, that he is just as like to spit on him and spurn him again. And Shylock's celebrated justification of his race runs headlong into a justification of his villainy: "The villainy which you teach me I will execute, and it shall go hard but I will better the instruction." "Hath not a Jew eyes?" and he proceeds to show that your Jew is no less than a man, and as such has a right, not to respect or compassion, as the critics for a century have had it, but to revenge. Neither large nor lofty are his claims. . . .

By all the devices, then, of Shakespeare's dramaturgy Shylock is proclaimed, as by the triple repetition of a crier, to be the villain, though a comic villain or butt. Nor does the poet let pass any of the prejudices of that day which might heighten this impression. A miser, a moneylender, a Jew—all three had from time immemorial been objects of popular detestation and ridicule, whether in life or on the stage. The union of them in one person is in Shakespeare's time the rule . . .: to the popular imagination a moneylender was a sordid miser with a hooked nose. So it is in the acknowledged prototype of Shylock, Marlowe's "bottle-nosed" monster, Barabas, the Jew of Malta. . . .

In the Elizabethan drama and character-writing, then, the Jew is both moneylender and miser, a villain who hankers after the Christian's blood, a gross egoist, even an atheist (though charged with dealings with the devil), and at the same time a butt, a hook-nosed niggard. And

2 I.iii.39f.; III.i.51.; III. iii. 2, 22f. [Stoll's note condensed].

a similar spirit of rude caricature and boisterous burlesque,
with even less of characterization, prevails, we have seen,
in the treatment of the Jew in early popular drama on the
Continent. Such is the soil from which the figure of Shylock
grew; for almost everything in Shakespeare is a growth,
and strikes root deep in the present and in the past, in
stage tradition and in the life about him.

The tradition having been examined, it now remains to
examine the opinions, or antipathies, of the time—a sorry
tale to tell. Critics have wondered at the knowledge of
Jewish character displayed by Shakespeare; but Sir Sidney
Lee some years since[3] showed that although banished from
England in 1290, and not readmitted until the latter days
of Cromwell, Jews were then not unknown. "Store of
Jewes we have in England," to quote *The Wandering Jew
Telling Fortunes to Englishmen* (1640); "a few in Court,
many in the Citty, more in the Countrey." In 1594, shortly
before *The Merchant of Venice* was written, one of these
Jews at court made something of a stir. Lopez, the Queen's
physician, was tried for conspiracy against her life. Sir
Sidney Lee has shown the bitterness of feeling which it
provoked, and the weight that was given to the fact that
the offender was a Jew by prosecutor, judges, and people.
"The perjured and murderous Jewish doctor," cried Coke,
"is worse than Judas himself"; and "of a religious profession," he said again, "fit for any execrable undertaking."
Even his judges spoke of him as "that vile Jew." Though
no longer a Jew by faith, when he protested from the
scaffold that "he loved the Queen as he loved Jesus Christ,"
such words "from a man of the Jewish profession," says
Camden, were "heard not without laughter"; and "He is

[3] *Gentleman's Magazine*, 1880, p. 187 f.; *Academy*, May 14, 1887;
Transactions of New Shakespeare Society, 1888. Commonly they followed
the trade of old-clothes dealer, it appears from a passage quoted by Sir
Sidney Lee from *Every Woman in her Humour* (1609), and from
Rowley's *Search for Money*, p. 15—as both now and in the days of
St. Jerome. Creizenach quotes Heywood's *Challenge for Beauty* (1635)
on their character: "Your English Jewes, they'le buy and sell their fathers,
prostrate their wives, and make money of their own children, the male
stewes can witnesse that." (*Works*, vol. v, 26.)

a Jew!" men cried aloud as the breath passed from his body. "And what's his reason?" asks Shylock in the play; "I am a Jew!"

Of itself this incident is enough to show that although there was by no means a Jewish peril in Shakespeare's day, the race-hatred of Angevin times had not burned out. Race-hatred, indeed, or the desire to profit by it, may have prompted the writing of this play, that Shakespeare's company might in the present excitement compete with Henslowe's in their *Jew of Malta*. Even the Reformation, in England as in Germany, had done little to quench it: only the later Puritans felt any relentings towards the chosen race. Hebrews of the Hebrews themselves, it was small wonder. The visionaries, the Fifth Monarchy men, the Root-and-Branch men, often looked almost kindly upon the Jews as they made the Jewish Sabbath henceforth and for ever the British Sabbath, contemplated surrounding Cromwell with a *Sanhedrim* of seventy councillors, and urged on Parliament the establishing of the *Torah* as the law of the realm. But the nation as a whole was not so minded; with it race-hatred went deeper than religion. Cromwell admitted the Jews in 1655; but it had to be, as Graetz remarks, by the back door, for the Commission designated to sit upon the measure was under the necessity of being admonished and dissolved like Parliament itself. Prynne, who for his own faith had lost his ears, wrote what was, measured by his own professional dissenter's standard, a *Short Demurrer*, in two parts, in which, like Luther a century before him, he raked up all the charges against the Jews that had ever been made, including usury, coining, cheating and oppression, crucifixion of children, blasphemy and sacrilege, malice towards man and God, the murder of Christ, obstinacy and hardness of heart. "Do not I hate them, O Lord, that hate thee?" he cries, with none to contradict him, in his zeal; "I hate them with a perfect hatred." And others there were like him, as appears from the petition to Parliament of Robert Rich, surnamed Mordecai, in 1653, on behalf of the Jews of England, Scotland, and Ireland: "Ever since 1648, it was hoped that persecution for conscience' sake would cease and truth and mercy take its place, but contrary thereto, these three last years hundreds in England have been cast into dungeons and prisons, some have perished, and others endured whippings, stonings, and spoilings of goods for matters concerning their law and conscience," etc. Even after these persecutions had, under Cromwell's iron hand, been allayed, and the Jews admitted to the rights of worship, it was upon a precarious basis. The doors of the first synagogue were threefold and double-locked. In 1660, a remonstrance upon their usurious and fraudulent practices was made by the Lord Mayor and Aldermen to the King, praying for the imposition on them of special taxes, seizure of their personal property, and banishment for residence without a license. Even after the Revolution, in 1689, a bill specially to tax the Jews was introduced into Parliament.

Such were the disabilities under which the Jews labored for a century after Shakespeare's day. What is the recorded opinion of his contemporaries? Coke, Solicitor-General, is comprehensible in abusing Lopez, but he is hardly so as, no longer Solicitor but a jurist, ex-Chief Justice of the King's Bench, he abuses the Jews in his *Institutes of the Laws of England.* "Odious," he calls them in his commentary on the *Statute De Judaismo,* "both to God and man;"—"these cruel Jews, wicked and wretched men." Bishop Joseph Hall, writing to Samuel Burton, Archdeacon of Gloucester, in 1607, rejoices that "our church is well rid of that accursed nation, whom yet Rome harbors . . . while instead of spitting at, or that their Neapolitan correction whereof Gratian speaks, the Pope solemnly receives at their hands that Bible which they at once approve and overthrow." He hates Rome for her tolerance and indulgence, forsooth. "The subtlest and most subdolous people," writes James Howell in 1633 to Lord Clifford; "the most hateful race of men." Jeremy Taylor thinks it is a wonder how the anger of God is gone out upon that miserable people. And Robert South, the greatest preacher in England a century after Shakespeare's death, declares, in a long and virulent passage, that it was appointed as the bitterest humiliation of Christ's life on earth that he should be born of the race of the Jews, "the most sordid and degenerate upon the earth." "And to this very day," he continues, "how much are they disgusted in all those kingdoms and dominions where they are dispersed! They are like dung upon the face of the earth; and that not so much for their being scattered as for being so offensive."

Nor is it a legal or theological prejudice merely. Popular literature, like the drama, is, as we have already seen, imbued with it; and dozens of ballads, like *Hugh of Lincoln* and *Gernutus,* still handed it down orally from generation to generation. Enlightenment prevailed not against it. . . . Frightful persecutions, the Jew-burnings, which at times of great emotional exaltation or depression raged through Europe in the thirteenth and fourteenth centuries, were almost always popular movements, not instigated or directed by the church; and princes, kings, emperors, popes like Clement VI, even fanatics like Saint Bernard, the Dominicans and the Franciscans, had, time and again, to interpose between the Jews and the violence of the mob. Converts fared little better than the faithful. And it was not the priest-ridden countries but those which first attained to a consciousness of national unity—England, France, Spain—as Wellhausen has shown, that expelled the Jews from their borders. In Italy, hard by the papal throne, they enjoyed greater security. In England, in the twentieth year of Henry III, the inhabitants of Southampton petitioned the king for a like privilege with the men of Newcastle, that no Jew should dwell amongst them, and Parliament granted Edward I a fifteenth in return for the favor of expelling the Jewish community as a whole. If, then, the hatred of Jews is at bottom a racial and social, rather than a religious, prejudice, and not Protestantism, not even the free thought of the Renaissance, but only Puritan fanaticism, late in the seventeenth century, availed, in any measure, to dispel it, why should we refuse to recognize it in Shakespeare, who, more than any other poet, reflected the settled prejudices and passions of his race?

To the Middle Ages, in the dearth of Jews and contemporary references to Jews in Elizabethan England, we must turn for illustration—but medieval is the sentiment of this comedy. Most readers and critics nowadays resent the despoiling of Shylock at the end. Indeed, where is there another instance of a villain in a Shakespearean comedy, with such cause for his villainy, coming off so ill? But even a century later, as we have seen, a sense of justice did not keep the government from the consideration of measures of confiscation and extra taxation; and all the European history of the Jewish race for a thousand years before is made up of such measures, put, without consideration, into effect. In the days of Titus, and afterwards in every nation and principality of Europe, they were *servi cameræ;* and, in return for the slight protection they thus received, they were pillaged and plundered, legally or illegally. Of his Jews every feudatory-in-chief spoke as of his serfs or his hounds; and he sold them, or bought them, or mortgaged them, or, like William Rufus waxed furious in defense of them, according to his needs. The king took possession of all the real property of which a Jew was seized, in case of his "death, outlawry, or departure hence" (or, in some parts of Europe, as soon, apparently, as he was known to have purchased it); and, in defiance of the fourth Lateran Council, of all property whatsoever, as the fruits of usury, on his conversion. *"Judæus vero nihil proprium habere potest,"* says Bracton (and the principle prevailed far beyond the Channel); *"quia quidquid acquirit non sibi acquirit sed regi, quia non vivunt sibi ipsis sed aliis, et sic aliis acquirunt et non sibi ipsis."* "They are doomed to perpetual servitude," writes Saint Thomas Aquinas, "and the lords of the earth may use their goods as their own." "The curse of the Patriarch rests upon the descendants of Ham," declared in 1851 the Supreme Court of Georgia, with reference to another subject race; "the Negro and his master are but fulfilling a divine appointment." A medieval sentiment, but alive in Shakespeare's day and not totally extinct in our own.

Nor were men content with injustice that was legal. . . . We do not forget that Shylock was also a usurer. Dr.

Honigmann, who is one of them that interpret *The Merchant of Venice* as a plea for toleration, says that in Shakespeare's day the word did not carry with it any stigma. Never, surely, was opinion more mistaken. By laws civil and ecclesiastical, usury—that is, the exaction of interest of any sort—was a crime. With expanding trade and manufacture the practice was widening, but was by no one approved in principle. By *37 Henry VIII, cap. ix,* the old laws against usury are, indeed, abolished, and a rate of ten percent is indirectly legalized by the fixing of severe penalties for any rate higher; but the practice is condemned, and classed with corrupt bargains. . . . In 1552, however, by *6 Edward VI, cap. xx,* the act of Henry VIII is annulled . . . and severe penalties are enacted against any usury whatever, "forasmuch as Usurie is by the word of God utterly prohibited, as a vyce most odyous and detestable. . . ." In 1570, by *13 Elizabeth, cap. viii, 6 Edward VI* is annulled and *37 Henry VIII* re-enacted, but "foreasmuch as all Usurie, being forbydden by the Law of God is synne and detestable," it ordains that even interest at ten percent or under is forfeitable. . . . It is expressly provided that all offenders shall "also be punished and corrected according to the ecclesiastical laws heretofore made against usury." . . .

[By another and earlier law of Elizabeth's reign, usury is one of the five crimes for which an offender may be subject to excommunication.]

Shylock was both moneylender and Jew. In him are embodied two of the deepest and most widely prevalent social antipathies of two thousand years, prevalent still, but in Shakespeare's day sanctioned by the teachings of religion besides. All that was religious in them Shakespeare probably shared like any other easygoing churchman; but all that was popular and of the people was part and parcel of his breath and blood. . . .

Those who will have it that Shylock, though bad, was made so, do violence to Shakespeare in two different ways. In the first place, they have recourse to an all-pervading irony. Antonio, gentlest and humblest of Shakespeare's

heroes, kicking and spitting at Jews and thrusting salvation down their throats,—such, they say, is the spectacle
of race-hatred pointed at by the poet. And those others
who will have it that Shylock is a noble spirit brought to
shame, carry the irony still further, into the characterization of Antonio and his friends. He, not Shylock, is the
caricature: his virtues are but affectations and shams; his
friends are parasites, spendthrifts, and fribbles! They
make no effort to raise the three thousand ducats to save
him, they do not even provide him with a surgeon against
his need.[4] That is, nothing is what it seems; a comedy
ending in moonlight blandishments and badinage is a tragedy, and the play written for the customers of the Globe
flies over their honest heads to the peaks of nineteenth-
century criticism. Irony is surely unthinkable unless the
author intends it, and here not the slightest trace of such
an intention appears. Moreover, a play of Shakespeare's is
self-contained; the irony is within it, so to speak, not under-
neath it. There is irony in the appearance of Banquo at
the moment when Macbeth presumes hypocritically to wish
for his presence at the feast; or, more obviously still, in the
fulfilment of the Witches' riddling oracles; but there is no
irony, as we have seen, such as Mr. Yeats discovers in the
success of Henry V and the failure of Richard II. There
is irony in the situation of a king so powerful reduced to a
state so pitiful, before he has "shook off the regal thoughts
wherewith he reigned"; but Shakespeare does not dream
that to fail and be a Richard is better than to succeed and
be a Henry—or an Antonio. He knows not the way of
thinking which lightly sets the judgment of the world aside,
nor the ways of modern artistic expression, which almost
withholds the purport of the higher judgment from the
world. No abysmal irony undermines his solid sense and
straightforward meaning. Shylock is indeed condemned;

---

4 These are only cases of neglect, which in Shakespeare abound. But
as I have said elsewhere, only the positive counts, or else the negative
made as prominent as the positive. On the stage—particularly the popular
and Shakespearean stage—it is what a man does, not what he leaves
undone, that makes the character; on the stage there are, so to speak, no
sins of omission.

Sir Henry Irving took no counsel of the poet when he made his exit from the ducal palace in pathetic triumph.

Nor is Jessica treated with malice, in mockery or irony, as, having forsaken him and robbed him and never since given him a regretful or pitying thought, she now revels in jest and sentiment, in moonlight and melody, at Belmont. . . . Signior Croce may be horrified at Jessica as was Rousseau at the unfilial Cléante; but just as sympathy at the theater traditionally is for the debtor and against the moneylender, so it is for the amorous son or eloping daughter and against the hard-hearted, stingy father. Thus it had been on the stage since the days of Plautus; cheating the old man was both sport for the slave and relief for the son's necessities. Either consideration gave pleasure in the comic theater. It is not ideal justice—that is not the business of comedy. . . .

In the second place, they do violence to Shakespeare, as Mr. Hudson observes, in representing Shylock as the product of his environment. The thoughts of men had hardly begun to run in such channels; the ancient rigors of retribution held fast; men still believed in heaven and hell, in villains and heroes. Though in Shakespeare there is little of George Eliot's moral austerity, as brought to bear on Tito Melema, for instance, Mr. Yeats errs, I think, in the opinion that his plays are, like all great literature, "written in the spirit of the Forgiveness of Sin." Macbeth is not forgiven, nor is Othello. Richard III and Iago were damned even in the making. Though the shortcomings of Falstaff, Bardolph, Pistol, and Nym serve a while as food for mirth, Shakespeare is in full accord with Henry V as he casts his fellows out of his company and out of his mind, to meet their end, maybe, in the brothel or on the gallows. And he is in full accord with Portia and the Duke in the judgment scene. Except in comedy, he has not the spirit of forgiveness which, like Uncle Toby's towards the Devil, comes of mere kindness of heart; and neither in comedy nor in tragedy has he the forgiveness of our psychological and social drama and novel, where both villains and heroes are no more, which comes of fullness of knowledge. Thus he deals with poverty, the hard-hearted, greasy,

foul-smelling, ignorant and ungrateful multitude, for which
he so often utters his aversion; and thus he deals with the
kindred subject of heredity. If a scoundrel is a bastard,
or is mean of birth, the fact is not viewed as an extenuat-
ing circumstance, but is turned to a reproach. It may in a
sense explain his depravity, but never explain it away. It
sets the seal upon it. It confirms the prejudice that there
is a difference between noble blood and that of low degree.
So, though our hearts are softened by Shylock's recital of
the indignities he has suffered, the hearts of the Elizabethans, by a simpler way of thinking, are hardened. It
confirms the prejudice that there is a difference betwixt
Christian and Jew. The Fathers, Protestant theologians
like Luther, seventeenth-century lawyers like Coke and
Prynne, review the pitiful story of the Jews in Europe
grimly, with at best a momentary and furtive pathos. It
proves their notion of the curse. . . .

With this conventionality in mind [i.e., that the under-
dog deserves his fate] we may approach the final question,
whether villain and [comic] butt as Shylock is, he may
not also be, as Professor Schelling thinks, a pathetic creation. As we have seen, he speaks of Shylock as "semi-
humorous," a character in whom there is a grotesqueness
bordering on laughter and a pathos bordering on tears.
The union of butt and villain is common in Shakespeare's
day, as old indeed as the stupid devils of the miracle-plays;
and the union of villain and droll goes back to the cleverer
devils, and the devils of Dante and medieval painting, and
underlies the characterization of most of the villains—
Aaron and Iago, for instance—in Shakespearean and
Elizabethan drama. But villain, butt, and pathetic figure,
all in one, is a thing difficult to conceive. . . .

Before, then, we take up this question whether Shylock
is also pathetic, we must consider some fundamental
principles, too much ignored: (1) That the interpretation
of literature—and of drama even more—is, as we have
seen, mainly a study in emphasis. (2) That much comedy
skirts the confines of tragedy, and what keeps it comedy
is emphasis, or a conventional "isolation," as Monsieur

Bergson has called it. (3) That comedy follows without question the manners and prejudices of the time. (4) That in the Shylock scenes there is so large an element of formal external comic technique that it is impossible to consider Shylock only "semi-humorous," in part pathetic. . . .

On the third principle we have been touching already. . . . This Rousseau pointed out long ago, and Monsieur Bergson has made it still clearer. The comic character is *"insocial,"* out of harmony with his social environment; and the spectator is kept *"insensible,"* unsympathetic—there, as Monsieur Bergson says, are two prerequisites. . . .

Now, in London there was no such refined society, or highly unified, organized, and sensitive social consciousness, as in Paris at the time of Molière, or in Athens at the time of Aristophanes; and Shakespeare, by temperament, was not a satirist; but nevertheless the comic spirit and method of all three dramatists had something in common, and the less refined the social consciousness, the more vindictive it is if aroused. Shakespeare's comedies are of course romantic, sentimental, and fanciful; but this contrast of low life with high life is one of his sources of comic effect as well; and honest but humble folk in *A Midsummer Night's Dream, Much Ado, As You Like It,* and *The Winter's Tale* are made almost unbelievably stupid and ridiculous, while those who in vanity aspire to rise above their appointed place and station, like Justice Shallow and Malvolio, are cheated or made the victims of a ruthless practical joke. Sir Toby, Maria, and the Clown sport with Malvolio while he howls in torment; and Autolycus, to the delight of himself and the audience, fleeces simple, trusting souls who have no fault save their rusticity. . . . But the most remarkable prejudice brought to bear for a comic effect in Shakespeare, is (as, from what has been said, might have been expected) not one which arises out of the *beau monde* at all but out of the people, society in the largest sense. It is the prejudice against Jew, miser, usurer. In each of these roles singly Shylock could not but be a purely repellent or comic figure on the stage because he was an object of derision in the street, indeed by tradition was on the stage as a comic figure already established;

and in these roles combined and united, not in a tragedy, but in a comedy, how could he possibly be thought pathetic at all?

. . . We here approach the last principle—the situation has been hedged about with the most explicitly comic technique and apparatus. . . . Here, quite apart from the social and racial prejudices . . . are the comic devices of repetition and inversion, as well as others less easily designated.

By repetition I mean, as in chapter IV, not the repetition of words or phrases at happy junctures . . . but the repetition of a *motif,* as in the daughter-ducats dialogue with Tubal, and in this case it takes the form of alternation:

> *Tubal.* One of them showed me a ring that he had of your daughter for a monkey.
> *Shylock.* Out upon her. Thou torturest me, Tubal. It was my turquoise; I had it of Leah when I was a bachelor. I would not have given it for a wilderness of monkeys.

This, most critics assert, the great historian [Creizenach] of the drama almost alone dissenting, is pathos: it is not the ducats behind the turquoise ("a diamond gone, cost me two thousand ducats in Frankfort!") but the thought of Leah that wrings his heart. "What a fine Hebraism is implied in this expression!" cries Hazlitt. "He has so deep a veneration for his dead wife," says Hawkins, with impenetrable gravity, "that a wilderness of monkeys would not compensate for the loss of the ring she had given him in youth." More Elizabethan fun running to waste! . . . Now he shrieks in grief for his ducats or his daughter, now in glee at Antonio's ruin. In his rage at the trading of a turquoise for a monkey, he blurts out, true to his native instincts, "not for a wilderness of monkeys!" and the Elizabethan audience, as well as some few readers today, have the heart—or the want of it—to think the valuation funny. . . .

Wrenched from the context, there are phrases, even

sentences, that may, indeed, seem pathetic. But Shakespeare, as soon as Tubal enters, lets Shylock strike up the
tune of "my daughter—my ducats," and, adhering to the
method of comic alternation throughout the scene, plays
the familiar dramatic trick of taking the audience in for
a moment and of then clapping upon the seemingly pathetic
sentiment a cynical, selfish, or simply incongruous one:

> Two thousand ducats in that; and other precious,
> precious jewels. I would my daughter were dead at my
> foot—and the jewels in her ear! Would she were hears'd
> at my foot—and the ducats in her coffin.

. . . The pathos is a pretense, a moment's illusion; the
laughter alone is real. Nor is it restrained—it is nothing
less than a roar. . . .

Then there is inversion, the tables turned. . . . The trial
scene is an example. . . .

Professor Baker holds that Shakespeare evinces a sense
of dramatic values in presenting Shylock's disappointment
as tragic in his own eyes, amusing in Gratiano's. How is
the tragic value presented? By the miser and usurer's prostrate prayer to the Duke to take his life if he would take
his wealth, or by the plea that he is not well? The biter
bitten, is the gibe cast at him at the end of *Il Pecorone;*
and that, exactly, is the spirit of the scene. . . . Shylock's
disappointment is tragic to him, but good care is taken that
it shall not be to us. Shakespeare is less intent on values
than on the conduct and direction of our sympathies
through the scene. This he manages both by the action
and the comment. The scene is a rise and a fall, a triumph
turned into a defeat, an apparent tragedy into a comedy;
and the defeat is made to repeat the stages of the triumph
so as to bring home to us the fact—the comic fact—of
retribution. When fortune turns, almost all the steps of the
ladder whereby Shylock with scales and knife had climbed
to clutch the fruit of revenge he must now descend empty-
handed and in bitterness; and what had been offered to
him and refused by him, he is now, when he demands it
again, refused. With the course of the action the comment

is in perfect accord and unison, marking and signalizing the stages of Shylock's fall. The outcries against the Jew and his stony heart, of the Duke, Bassanio, and Gratiano—protested against by Antonio as futile—give place to the jeers of Gratiano and the irony of the fair judge. Gratiano is not the only one to crow. "Thou shalt have justice, more than thou desir'st—Soft! The Jew shall have all justice—Why doth the Jew pause? Take thy forfeiture—Tarry, Jew; the law hath yet another hold on you—Art thou contented, Jew? What dost thou say?" Aimed at Shylock as he pleads and squirms, these words fall from lips which had a moment before extolled the heavenly qualities of mercy! But for more than the meager mercy which Shylock is shown there is neither time nor place, the crowing fits the latter part of the action as perfectly as the indignant comment had fitted the earlier, and we must equally accept it or divest the scene of meaning and sense. The Jew's very words are echoed by Portia and Gratiano as they jeer, and at every turn that the course of justice takes (welcomed by Shylock, while in his favor, with hoarse cries of gloating and triumph) there are now peals and shouts of laughter, such laughter as arises when Tartuffe the hypocrite is caught by Orgon—"*un rire se lève de tous les coins de la salle, un rire de vengeance si vous voulez, un rire amer, un rire violent.*" The running fire assails him to the very moment—and beyond it—that Shylock says he is not well, and staggers out, amid Gratiano's jeers touching his baptism, to provoke in the audience the laughter of triumph and vengeance in his own day and bring tears to their eyes in ours. How can we here for a moment sympathize with Shylock unless at the same time we indignantly turn, not only against Gratiano, but against Portia, the Duke, and all Venice as well?

LINDA BAMBER

The Avoidance of Choice: A Woman's Privilege

The one woman in the comedies whose marriage actually does involve a betrayal of her father is Jessica. Two things, however, distinguish her choice from that of the women in the tragedies: first, it is so lightheartedly made that we hardly perceive it as a choice; and second, Shylock is such a villain that we rarely take his feelings into account. The following exchange is illustrative of both Jessica's insouciance and the general assumption in *The Merchant of Venice* that Shylock is a dreadful person:

> *Launcelot* ... look you, the sins of the father are to be laid upon the children. ... you may partly hope that your father got you not—that you are not the Jew's daughter.
> *Jessica* That were a kind of bastard hope indeed! So the sins of my mother should be visited upon me.
> *Launcelot* Truly then, I fear you are damned both by father and mother. Thus when I shun Scylla your father, I fall into Charybdis your mother. Well, you are gone both ways.
>
> (III.v.1–18)

In this fantasy the betrayal of Shylock is pushed back a generation from Jessica to her mother; Jessica is thoroughly justified in her desertion of her father; and the whole issue is cheerfully dismissed in Jessica's last remark: "I

From *Comic Women, Tragic Men* by Linda Bamber. (Stanford, Calif.: Stanford University Press, 1982), pp. 117–20.

shall be saved by my husband. He hath made me a Christian" (III.v.19–20). In this exchange heavy themes are orchestrated very lightly; salvation and damnation are subjects for witty repartee. Similarly, the theme of the betrayed father is so lightheartedly developed as to defuse anxieties even as it provokes them.

Furthermore, Shylock and Jessica are not the only father and daughter in the play. They are only the father and daughter appropriate to Venice, to realism, to the world of hard choices. The late Duke of Belmont and Portia present the Belmont version of the father-daughter theme. Portia's father has left a will that would seem to require her to choose between love and family loyalty. But whereas Jessica actually makes such a choice, Portia is spared the trouble of doing so. Her will *happens* to coincide with the terms of her father's will. . . . Jessica's betrayal of Shylock is balanced by the happy outcome of Portia's obedience to her father's will.

How are we to understand the feminine avoidance of choice in Shakespeare's comedies? On the one hand it may seem to depotentiate the women; the comic heroine may seem a masculine wish-fulfillment, an Other who may be loved at no risk to the Self. But on the other hand, the avoidance of choice is a positive gift and a comic prerogative. In the world of comedy the barriers are lowered between our alternatives, and it is the characters who take advantage of the situation that appeal to us most. In *A Midsummer Night's Dream,* for instance, the barrier is temporarily lowered between the world of reality and the world of the imagination. Bottom appeals to us because he moves with such aplomb between the real and the fantastic, stepping over the barriers as if they were not there. This is what we long to do in comedy: *not* to choose between competing worlds but to move between them with Bottom's stupendous calm. In tragedy, of course, the situation is different. In tragedy our alternatives are mutually exclusive, and characters who refuse to choose between them write themselves out of the story. Octavia and Ophelia, for instance, are much reduced by their failures to choose between men—Antony and Caesar in Octavia's case, and

Hamlet and Polonius in Ophelia's. In tragedy we reserve our admiration for those who face their choices squarely, like Cordelia and Desdemona. But in comedy we are attracted to characters who minister to our sense of freedom from choice, and it is no coincidence that these characters are often women. It is the feminine Other who is most at home in the alternative world; the male Self, as we shall see, is less than brilliant in this setting. Bottom is an exception, a male character whose presence dissolves all oppositions; but Bottom is hardly a male Self. His unconsciousness (not to say stupidity) makes him Other to the reader just as his lack of social status makes him Other to the Athenian lovers. When the feminine Other represents the avoidance of choice she does so more consciously than Bottom —although not necessarily more appealingly.

In *The Merchant of Venice,* for instance, Portia spares us the choice between love and law, Belmont and Venice, stepping Bottomlike over the barriers between the two worlds. Just as Bottom goes from being a real tinker to being an imaginary ass-headed creature, Portia goes from being a Belmont heiress to being a Venetian judge. But Bottom is at home in the world of the fantastic because he refuses to dwell on its differences from ordinary life. Portia, on the other hand, is at home in Venice because she knows exactly what the differences are between this public world and the world she has come from. She is perfectly conscious of the choices that face us in this play; she is merely confident that they need not be made.

In this play, general philosophical choices arise from specific choices made by the male hero, Bassanio. Bassanio is faced with a conflict between his concern for his friend and his own desire to marry Portia. He chooses Portia, allows Antonio to become bound to Shylock, and is about to suffer the consequences when Portia sweeps into Venice and saves him from them. At the same time she saves *us* from the philosophical choice between love and law. Because of her, we do not have to choose between our desire for social order and our desire to see our representative excused from society's bargains. On the one hand,

> The duke cannot deny the course of law;
> For the commodity that strangers have
> With us in Venice, if it be denied,
> Will much impeach the justice of the state,
> Since that the trade and profit of the city
> Consisteth of all nations.
>
> (III.iii.26–31)

In other words, it will be bad for business, bad for all our business, if Antonio is let off from his bond. But on the other hand, Antonio is a good man, a dear friend, and does not deserve to die at Shylock's hands. The conflict is absolute; when Portia arrives from Belmont it simply melts away. The course of law is upheld *and* Antonio is saved; because of the comic heroine we can have things both ways.

In Shakespearean comedy the successful avoidance of choice is a feminine prerogative, and the men are burdened with a graceless tendency to choose. During Antonio's trial, for instance, Bassanio blunders into this strange speech:

> Antonio, I am married to a wife
> Which is as dear to me as life itself;
> But life itself, my wife, and all the world
> Are not with me esteemed above thy life.
> I would lose all, ay sacrifice them all,
> Here to this devil, to deliver you.
>
> (IV.i.281–86)

In a passion to show his friendship for Antonio, Bassanio offers up his love for Portia, gratuitously creating a conflict between the two. No one has demanded the sacrifice of Portia, nor is it clear how it could possibly be of any help. Portia, in disguise as Bellario, is understandably annoyed to hear her husband say these lines. She tells him coolly, "Your wife would give you little thanks for that/If she were by to hear you make the offer." In mock revenge, Portia later pretends to have sacrificed Bassanio to a figure from his own public life: "Pardon me, Bassanio,/For by this ring the doctor lay with me" (V.i.258–59). Of course, Portia herself is the "doctor." As Bellario she demands the ring from Bassanio; as Portia she produces the ring to prove her own infidelity. The point is Bassanio's failure to be two things at once as Portia has been. Since he has betrayed her by choosing between love and friendship, she pretends to have betrayed him by choosing between men. The contrast is striking between the two characters at this moment. Bassanio seems heavy, puzzled, slightly unfit for the world of comedy; he has chosen Portia over Antonio, Antonio over Portia, and now he wants Portia again. Each time he has clumsily identified himself with a single desire. Portia, on the other hand, is talented and desirous as both a woman and a man, Bassanio's wife and, as it were, his lawyer. It is the feminine Other who can avoid choice in comedy, who can perform alternative identities, who can move gracefully between worlds that the hero finds mutually exclusive. The male Self seems tainted in the world of comedy by the lingering necessity to choose. He expects to be one thing only, like a tragic hero; in comedy we are blessedly free to be this and that, or both at once.

In the courtroom scene, Bassanio fabricates a conflict where none exists; but the comic hero's choice is not always unnecessary. The typical choice faced by the hero in comedy is the one between love and friendship, between a woman and a man. But with the exception of *A Midsummer Night's Dream*, no play deals with a conflict for women between friendship and love. The final word on female friendship comes in *The Merry Wives of Windsor* when Mr. Ford derides the intimacy between Mrs. Page and his wife. Mr. Ford tells Mrs. Page, "I think if your husbands were dead, you two would marry," and Mrs. Page snaps back, "Be sure of that—two other husbands" (III.ii.13–15). Marriage is marriage; friendship is friendship. The feminine Other is confident she may simultaneously enjoy relationships that may be mutually exclusive for the male Self.

ALEXANDER LEGGATT

The Fourth and Fifth Acts

[Portia's] disguise gives her, like Julia, a masculine freedom of action. But at first she comes to Venice speaking
the accents of Belmont, conditioned by the world of easy
wealth she has always known. She opposes the free bounty
of mercy to Shylock's hard demand for justice:

> The quality of mercy is not strained;
> It droppeth as the gentle rain from heaven
> Upon the place beneath.
>
> (IV.i.183–85)

But the result of this plea is the most serious instance yet
of the device by which a speech is addressed to an uncom-
prehending listener. Portia speaks of God, heaven and, at
the lowest level, of thronèd monarchs. But Shylock is
resolutely a creature of the earth. The most detailed reference he has made to his own tradition is a story of copu-
lating rams. When he speaks of our common humanity, it
is in physical terms: "If you prick us, do we not bleed?
If you tickle us, do we not laugh?" (III.i.61–2). He seeks
even his revenge in the most crudely physical terms. Portia's speech on mercy has an easy flow, but its images are
somewhat disembodied.[1] Shylock, as is frequently remarked, hoards his words.[2] but his language is as concrete
as the scraping sound of the knife on his shoe, and he
illustrates his arguments with pungent coarseness:

From *Shakespeare's Comedy of Love* by Alexander Leggatt. (London: Methuen, 1974), pp. 137–50.

[1] See Clifford Leech, *The Dramatist's Experience* (London, 1970),
pp. 158–9.

[2] See Mark Van Doren, *Shakespeare* (New York, 1939), p. 101; and
Theodore Weiss, *The Breath of Clowns and Kings* (London, 1971),
p. 126.

> Some men there are love not a gaping pig;
> Some that are mad if they behold a cat;
> And others, when the bagpipe sings i'th' nose,
> Cannot contain their urine. . . .

> (IV.i.47–50)

Portia and Shylock speak with utterly opposing voices; there can be no meeting of minds between them. Her plea for mercy may have won the hearts of the anthologists, but for all the effect it has on Shylock she might as well not have spoken. He cannot be cracked from outside, for his implacable "humor," as he himself describes it (IV.i.43), is its own justification, a closed circle of logic—"Hates any man the thing he would not kill?" (IV.i.67)—to which no other standard is relevant.

Portia, like Bassanio, must now answer a riddle: she must enter the mind of her adversary, just as Bassanio entered the mind of her dead father and saw the inner logic of the casket game. According to Thomas Marc Parrott, "In Portia's decision we see the triumph of the spirit over the letter, of equity over legalism."[8] We see, I think, something more painful and alarming than that. When her appeal to mercy fails, Portia begins to test Shylock, as the caskets had tested her unwanted suitors. In a series of exchanges she establishes that he will not take the money, that he has no surgeon by to stanch the blood (" 'tis not in the bond"—IV.i.261), and that he does have the balances to weigh the flesh: in short, that he takes his bond logically and literally, as Morocco and Arragon took the casket mottoes logically and literally. Very well, then: there is one piece of logic he has overlooked. She will use the letter to defeat the letter. When she gives her judgment there is a new tone in her voice, a cold remorseless logic, with a leaden thump on the key words:

> This bond doth give thee here no jot of blood:
> The words expressly are "a pound of flesh."
> Take then thy bond, take thou thy pound of flesh;
> But, in the cutting of it, if thou dost shed

[8] *Shakespearean Comedy* (New York, 1949), p. 139.

One drop of Christian blood, thy lands and goods
Are, by the laws of Venice, confiscate
Unto the state of Venice.

                                        (IV.i.305–11)

She follows up her argument in detail, releasing one by
one the full terrors of the law that Shylock had invoked,
playing Shylock's own game with a deadly thoroughness
that is more than a little alarming. She does in a more
purposeful way what Gratiano does more shallowly by
flinging Shylock's own words back at him. She leaves it to
Gratiano to show triumph, and to the Duke and Antonio
to show mercy: she reserves for herself only the impersonal
accents of the law. In place of the flowing bounty of her
earlier speeches we hear, at the climax of her argument,
the hard command: "Down, therefore, and beg mercy of
the Duke" (IV.i.362). Mercy no longer flows freely: it has
to be begged, as Shylock made Antonio and his friends
beg. As Bassanio entered and understood the conventions
of Belmont, Portia has now entered and understood the
special conventions of Shylock's mind, the diabolical game
of "justice." And she destroys Shylock with the weapon
most fatal to convention—parody.

But—apart from the strange moment when Shylock first
proposed the bond—we had not previously thought of
Venice as a particularly conventionalized world, certainly
not when compared with Belmont. It seemed, if less con-
genial, more natural and realistic. In this respect, however,
the balance of the play has now shifted: Venice, in the
trial scene, has become a formal world where a simple
dramatic issue is at stake. As in the earlier Belmont scenes,
a riddle must be solved. We still hear a wide range of
voices, from the tense authority of the Duke to the savagery of Gratiano, but the speed and fluidity are gone, and
the sense of busy traffic is stilled as a single crucial issue is
decided. The enclosure of the action in the court—something new for the Venetian scenes—adds to this effect.
Belmont, on the other hand, has acquired a more open
and natural dramatic idiom in the immediately preceding
scenes, beginning with the arrival of the messengers from

Venice. Portia's preparations for her journey have some of the haste and bustle of Bassanio's preparations in the earlier scenes:

> Take this same letter,
> And use thou all th'endeavor of a man
> In speed to Padua; see thou render this
> Into my cousin's hands, Doctor Bellario;
> And look what notes and garments he doth give thee,
> Bring them, I pray thee, with imagined speed
> Unto the traject, to the common ferry
> Which trades to Venice.
>
> (III.iv.47–54)

And just before the trial we have that casual, inconsequential scene with Lorenzo, Jessica and Lancelot. Lancelot's jokes, the preparations for dinner, the seemingly irrelevant detail of the Moor's pregnancy (and where did *she* come from, by the way?)—all these combine to suggest a natural world, going about its independent business, far from the passions of the courtroom.

There may also be, in that scene, some ironic foreshadowing of the trial. Lancelot's complaint that "This making of Christians will raise the price of hogs" (III.v.22) may refer forward to Shylock, as well as backward to Jessica. More important, some of Lancelot's joking depends on the excessively literal interpretation of words. Lorenzo remarks,

> I do know
> A many fools that stand in better place,
> Garnished like him, that for a tricksy word
> Defy the matter.
>
> (III.v.66–69)

This is followed immediately by Jessica's praise of Portia; yet we will soon see Portia play Lancelot's game in a far more serious way. These touches, light though they are, may have a slight distancing effect if we can remember them in the trial scene itself, since they place some of the

key motifs of that scene in a context that trivializes them.
But there is a more daring effect, right at the heart of the
trial scene. Portia has just told Antonio to prepare for
death, and he and Bassanio are taking a last farewell. The
crisis is nearly upon us, when we hear the following:

BASSANIO: Antonio, I am married to a wife
           Which is as dear to me as life itself;
           But life itself, my wife, and all the world
           Are not with me esteemed above thy life;
           I would lose all, ay, sacrifice them all
           Here to this devil, to deliver you.
  PORTIA: Your wife would give you little thanks for that,
           If she were by to hear you make the offer.
GRATIANO: I have a wife who I protest I love;
           I would she were in heaven, so she could
           Entreat some power to change this currish Jew.
 NERISSA: 'Tis well you offer it behind her back;
           The wish would make else an unquiet house.
 SHYLOCK: (Aside) These be the Christian husbands! I have a
                                                     daughter—

           Would any of the stock of Barrabas
           Had been her husband, rather than a Christian!
                                              (IV.i.281–95)

Like Salerio's arrival in Belmont, this exchange jolts us out
of our involvement with the immediate business of the
scene, and forces us to see it in a larger context. But here
the effect is reversed: we are pulled away from the suffering of the courtroom and reminded of the more comic
world of love. As Bassanio speaks, his earnest manner is
compromised by our growing realization of the irony of
his making the offer in Portia's presence. The effect of his
speech hovers between serious concern and laughter; but
in the comic symmetry of the following exchanges, and
the wry abruptness of the women's replies (especially
Nerissa's), the balance quickly tilts toward laughter. Even
Shylock makes a joke of it, though his joke is more bitter
and takes us back eventually to the serious business of the

scene. The defeat of Shylock comes only a few lines later; but this passage has already put us at a slight distance from the trial, and lessened (though not destroyed) the seriousness of our involvement with it, by reminding us that there is a world elsewhere.

It is as well that the trial is thus slightly distanced and conventionalized: it helps us to remember that Portia, in out-Shylocking Shylock, is adopting a necessary but temporary role, not showing us her true face. There is something not only unclean but unreal about the trial, both in Shylock's demand and in the manner of his defeat. At the heart of the casket game is human reality, reassuringly ordinary and familiar. There is, in the grimmer game that Shylock plays, human reality of a different kind, his deep need for vengeance on Antonio; but to satisfy that need he depends on an impersonal, logical principle, which is no respecter of persons, and which can be used just as easily against Shylock as for him. Portia, in her grim parody of Shylock, shows us what "justice" really looks like when it is taken to its logical conclusion. It is a mad obsession with precision:

> if thou tak'st more
> Or less than a just pound—be it but so much
> As makes it light or heavy in the substance,
> Or the division of the twentieth part
> Of one poor scruple; nay, if the scale do turn
> But in the estimation of a hair—
> Thou diest, and all thy goods are confiscate.
> (IV.i.325–31)

The freeflowing generosity of Portia's normal speech— "Pay him six thousand, and deface the bond; / Double six thousand, and then treble that" (III.ii.301–2)—is sharply reversed, and becomes an obsession with increasingly minute measurement. This is more truly fantastic than anything in the Belmont scenes: like some of the more unsettling fantasies of Lewis Carroll, it shows what happens when logical principles are set to work without the restraints of humanity and common sense. If we are to emerge from the play with any feeling of reassurance at all, we need to feel—as I think we do—that this mad trial is not a final vision of human reality.

All the same, Shylock's hate is real enough, however fantastic the manner in which he has tried to satisfy it. And that hate has merely been defeated, not dissipated. The mercy shown him by the Duke and Antonio makes no more impression on him than Portia's abstract appeal had done. Moreover, while Shylock can be ordered off the stage, he remains an immovable part of the play's vision: he is too vigorous and convincing a figure to be brushed aside with a wave of the hand, like Egeus, and quickly forgotten. In fact, we need to remember him if the final scene is to have its full effect. I have already remarked on the exclusiveness—indeed, the privateness—of the comic finale, and I think the vision of harmony it offers is carefully and deliberately restricted. It is right that it should be so, for the play as a whole has shown an uncomfortable world where hate breeds easily and where even love makes painful demands.

Toward the end of *Love's Labor's Lost* and *A Midsummer Night's Dream* there were passages in which the play's central vision was stated in objective terms, apart from the immediate concerns of the characters: the songs of Spring and Winter, an image of mutability, and the description of Theseus's hounds, an image of harmony. At the start of Act V of *The Merchant of Venice,* there is a similar but longer and more elaborate passage. It may seem odd at first glance that Lorenzo and Jessica, so unsatisfying as purely romantic lovers, should be chosen to deliver a rhapsody on the beauty of the night, the music of the spheres and the power of harmony. But that is just the point. In their scene at Belmont just before the trial, they have established a special conversational technique by which, while praising the perfections of others, they joke about their own distance from perfection. Jessica says of Portia:

Why, if two gods should play some heavenly match,
And on the wager lay two earthly women,
And Portia one, there must be something else
Pawned with the other; for the poor rude world
Hath not her fellow.

LORENZO: Even such a husband
Hast thou of me as she is for a wife.

JESSICA: Nay, but ask my opinion too of that.

LORENZO: I will anon; first let us go to dinner.

JESSICA: Nay, let me praise you while I have a stomach.

(III.v.79–86)

As soon as they discuss themselves, they become chatty
and ironic. And through the opening passage of Act V they
teasingly set themselves against higher, unattainable ideals.
Their first exchange, on tragic stories of love, is patterned
and graceful, but its very patterning makes those tragic
tales seem remote. The passage thus creates a comic exor-
cism of the tragic side of love, recalling the technique of
A Midsummer Night's Dream (in fact one of the tales is
that of Pyramus and Thisbe). Then, using the same patterned dialogue (and burlesquing it in the process) they
descend from these high, remote tales of sorrow and infidelity to a joking accusation of infidelity here and now:

LORENZO: In such a night
Did Jessica steal from the wealthy Jew,
And with an unthrift love did run from Venice,
As far as Belmont.

JESSICA: In such a night
Did young Lorenzo swear he loved her well,
Stealing her soul, with many vows of faith,
And ne'er a true one.

LORENZO: In such a night
Did pretty Jessica, like a little shrew,
Slander her love, and he forgave it her.

JESSICA: I would out-night you, did no body come;
But, hark, I hear the footing of a man.

(V.i.14–24)

The pattern is mocked, and then broken. As in the depiction of Portia's three suitors, we descend from the remote and exotic to the immediate and human—though here the descent is not so much reassuring as sharply comic. There can be a sadness, too, in this descent: Lorenzo's next meditation, on the music of the spheres, is less stylized, more earnest in tone and admits the imperfections of the here and now with deeper regret:

> Such harmony is in immortal souls,
> But whilst this muddy vesture of decay
> Doth grossly close it in, we cannot hear it.
>
> (V.i.63–5)

When comedy measures itself against the world of tragedy it can mock it easily enough, for its own vision is essentially different. But beyond tragedy is the vision of permanent, immutable harmony—a vision that is closer to comedy's own concerns; and here there is a deeper sadness in measuring the distance between two imperfect human lovers and the principle of love that orders the universe.

That is as much as Lorenzo and Jessica can give us; but they have seen in Portia a vision of perfection in human terms. And when Portia herself enters the argument is taken one step further:

PORTIA: That light we see is burning in my hall.
How far that little candle throws his beams!
So shines a good deed in a naughty world.
NERISSA: When the moon shone, we did not see the candle.
PORTIA: So doth the greater glory dim the less:
A substitute shines brightly as a king
Until a king be by, and then his state
Empties itself, as doth an inland brook
Into the main of waters. Music! hark!
NERISSA: It is your music, madam, of the house.
PORTIA: Nothing is good, I see, without respect;
Methinks it sounds much sweeter than by day.
NERISSA: Silence bestows that virtue on it, madam.

PORTIA: The crow doth sing as sweetly as the lark
When neither is attended; and I think
The nightingale, if she should sing by day,
When every goose is cackling, would be thought
No better a musician than the wren.
How many things by season season'd are
To their right praise and true perfection!

(V.i.89-108)

The importance of context, so vital a part of Shakespeare's comic technique, is here argued explicitly by one of his characters. Context can be used in a variety of ways; but here Portia's argument is that placing too great a beauty against a lesser one, measuring ourselves against standards that are too high, is unjustly belittling, and may blind us to the real beauty of the lesser light. If we concentrate on each experience for its merits, we may find beauty even from the most unlikely sources. (The merry owl of *Love's Labor's Lost* was mildly surprising; here we are asked to think of a sweetly-singing crow!) The argument is confirmed by the atmosphere of the scene as a whole, in which constant references to the beauty of the night and the charm of the music combine to create an image of the harmony that can be achieved even in the fallen world.

This passage, with its hard-won but steady idealism, is still generalized; indeed we may feel that it achieves its confidence only by keeping off the problems of the characters themselves; and the more boisterous, bawdy fun of the ring sequence may seem like a descent to crude realities, away from the vision of harmony. But the ideal is not totally disembodied. It is centered on Portia, the figure of the greatest range and authority in the play: the candle shines from her house; it is her music that sounds, And I suspect that in the ring sequence Portia is applying her attitude of acceptance to the most difficult unresolved dilemma remaining in the play—the conflicting loyalties of Bassanio. The ring embodies those conflicting loyalties: it is Portia's wedding ring, given away at Antonio's insistence, as a sign that his gratitude for his friend's safety outweighs his wife's command:

> My Lord Bassanio, let him have the ring.
> Let his deservings, and my love withal,
> Be valued 'gainst your wife's commandment.
>
> (IV.i.448–50)

The conflicting demands on Bassanio have been at the bottom of the most striking moments of dislocation in the play, when Salerio brought Antonio's letter to Belmont, and when Portia and Nerissa spoke up for themselves as wives, at the crisis of the trial scene. The whole idea of obligation has been a painful one, conveyed in images of bodily torture:

> Here is a letter, lady,
> The paper as the body of my friend,
> And every word in it a gaping wound
> Issuing life-blood.
>
> (III.ii.263–6)

The image is rooted in Antonio's grisly debt to Shylock, incurred in serving Bassanio—who wishes at one point that he could repay the debt in similar terms: "The Jew shall have my flesh, blood, bones and all, / Ere thou shalt lose for me one drop of blood" (IV.i.112–13). The same imagery is used when Portia lectures Gratiano for having given away his ring, which, she says, was "riveted with faith unto your flesh" (V.i.169). Bassanio, not liking the turn of the conversation, exclaims aside "Why, I were best to cut my left hand off, / And swear I lost the ring defending it" (V.i.177–8). But here the tone is lighter; and throughout the final scene we are made to see the comic side of Bassanio's dilemma. The dialogue is patterned and repetitive, Gratiano and Nerissa add their usual comic symmetry, and when the women claim to have slept with the youths who had the rings, the laughter becomes broad and earthy. As we saw in the trial scene, there was always a comic potential in the conflicting demands on Bassanio, and when he is finally made to face that conflict, a comic idiom is used. There are one or two hints of serious feeling, as in Bassanio's pained recollection, "I was beset with shame and courtesy" (V.i.217), but for the most part the technique is that of the lovers' quarrel in *A Midsummer Night's Dream*, keeping us at a distance from the pain of the dilemma by emphasizing the neatness of its pattern.[4]

We know, too, that Bassanio's dilemma, so far as it is represented by the giving of the ring, is more apparent than real. He gave Portia's ring to Portia, and the revelation of this provides a neat comic resolution. Without wishing to be too solemn about it, one may suggest that the solution to the comic problem points to a way of resolving the deeper emotional dilemma: there is no final contradiction between Bassanio's ties with Portia and his ties with Antonio. It is the capacity to love that matters, and love can extend itself beyond a single person. This was suggested earlier in the play, when Portia saw her obligation to Antonio (whom she had never seen) as an extension of her love for Bassanio. Being close friends, she argued, the two men must be similar:

> Which makes me think that this Antonio,
> Being the bosom lover of my lord,
> Must needs be like my lord. If it be so,
> How little is the cost I have bestowed
> In purchasing the semblance of my soul
> From out the state of hellish cruelty!
>
> (III.iv.16–21)

In the final scene, it is Antonio who gives the ring back to Bassanio, suggesting, emblematically, that he has a share in their happiness.[5] In this way, a personal, emotional

---

[4] In Terry Hands's production for the Royal Shakespeare Company in 1971, an attempt was made to present the ring sequence as a serious emotional dilemma (for example, when Bassanio parted with the ring, Portia burst into tears). But all through the last scene, there was a distinct feeling that the actors were fighting the natural rhythm of the dialogue, and I think the experiment, interesting though it was, demonstrated that the normal comic reading, which usually works so well, is in fact the right one.

[5] See Hyman, "The rival lovers," *Shakespeare Quarterly* 21 (1970), 113. At the end of Sonnet XLII a similar solution is proposed to the love triangle: "But here's the joy: my friend and I are one;/Sweet flattery! then she loves but me alone." But here the solution is presented with obvious irony, as a rhetorical trick that carries no real consolation.

dilemma is transformed into a comic plot design, lightened
and conventionalized; and in the process its pain is dissipated and it becomes an occasion for happiness. Portia's
general idea of seeking happiness in the here and now,
even in the most unlikely places, is here applied in
practice.

But we are also aware, I think, that happiness can be
drawn out of such a situation only if its implications are
carefully limited. Antonio's quiet manner in the final scene
—"I am th'unhappy subject of these quarrels" (V.i.238)
—does not suggest a joyful acceptance of his role in the
emblematic pattern of harmony. The sexual joking of
Gratiano's final speech narrows the implications of love to
the two pairs of lovers going off to bed, and Antonio can
have no part in this. The restoration of his galleys is an
event so mysterious and remote that it carries no emotional weight to match the very real anxiety of his earlier
losses:

> PORTIA: . . . Unseal this letter soon;
> There you shall find three of your argosies
> Are richly come to harbor suddenly.
> You shall not know by what strange accident
> I chanced on this letter.
> ANTONIO: I am dumb.
>
> (V.i.275-9)

There is no direct statement that Antonio is still unhappy,
though an actor can suggest this.[6] But the stage is domi-
nated by four lovers (six, if we count Lorenzo and Jessica), and he is the odd man out. Moreover, the satisfactions
he is given are so conventionalized that we cannot be sure
how much weight they carry in personal terms—very little,
if we are to judge by his reticent manner: the character
seems a little detached from the conventional pattern in
which he is placed. As in *A Midsummer Night's Dream*,
the harmony of the comic ending must be achieved by

----

6 Tyrone Guthrie's production at Stratford, Ontario in 1955 ended
with Antonio alone on stage, still holding the letter with the news of
his galleys. As the lights faded, he let the paper fall.

selection; Portia's speeches about finding beauty by shutting out distractions have suggested as much. But while in the other play we were only *told* what had been left out, here we are shown. The play includes many characters—notably Shylock—who have no part in the final scene. Antonio is on stage, but his involvement is limited and his share in the lovers' harmony is dubious. And the comic stylization of the ring sequence, though it functions effectively on its own terms, involves a narrowing of the play's stylistic and emotional range. In short, the play has shown a larger world than it can finally bring into harmony. This sense of instability is reflected in the dramatic idiom. The play's ultimate gamble, I have suggested, is to combine conventionalized action with human reality, naturalistically conceived. This combination produces shifting, unpredictable results, from the trust in convention in the casket scenes to the distaste of the trial scene, in which the conventionalized action suggests an unhealthy narrowing of vision. In the end Shakespeare pulls back from some of the new territory he has explored: the ring sequence, with its patterned teams of lovers, recalls *Love's Labor's Lost* and *A Midsummer Night's Dream* in its comically stylized presentation of the games of romantic love. It presents, in a now familiar way, an image of order coming from apparent disorder: it is a standard comic ending. But such an ending is itself a convention, and in *The Merchant of Venice* that convention, for all its power, is allowed only a limited success in bringing order out of an intractable world. The security the lovers attain is, like the candle that shines from Portia's house, "a good deed in a naughty world," an area of private happiness for those who can achieve it. The gamble of wedding complex characters to formalized action is exciting, but the combination is too volatile to allow more than a limited sense of harmony at the end.

The Merchant of Venice on the Stage

This is the Jew
That Shakespeare drew.

(doggerel lines, attributed to
Alexander Pope, on Charles Macklin's performance)

Probably most actors who play the role of Shylock believe that they are true to the text, and yet we have reports of a wide range of Shylocks. Moreover, exactly what does one mean when one says that a certain portrayal renders the figure "that Shakespeare drew"? In the absence of any explicit statement by Shakespeare about his intention, how can we tell? And even if we had some sort of explicit statement, how could we be certain that we should trust it? If Shakespeare had told his fellow actors that Shylock proposes the bond only "in a merry sport" (as Shylock says in I.iii.142), would we be compelled to believe him, any more than if he told them that some of his best friends were Jews? (There was indeed a colony of Jews in Shakespeare's London, though outwardly they professed Christianity.) Would we not protest that earlier in the scene, in an aside, Shylock says of Antonio, "If I can catch him once upon the hip, / I will feed fat the ancient grudge I bear him"?

Such a passage pretty clearly suggests that Shylock is waiting for his chance to destroy Antonio, and in trying to find "the Jew / That Shakespeare drew" we can only look at this passage and all of the other passages that go to make up the whole of The Merchant of Venice. If we look at the whole play, we will find many passages that suggest a villainous Shylock. And yet we will also find this:

I am a Jew. Hath not a Jew eyes? Hath not a Jew hands,
organs, dimensions, senses, affections, passions?—fed
with the same food, hurt with the same weapons, subject
to the same diseases, healed by the same means, warmed
and cooled by the same winter and summer as a Christian
is? If you prick us, do we not bleed? If you tickle us,
do we not laugh? If you poison us, do we not die? And
if you wrong us, shall we not revenge? If we are like
you in the rest, we will resemble you in that.

(III.i.55–65)

Different actors have emphasized different passages in the
play, and thus have arrived at different interpretations.
Moreover, different ages inevitably must see the play in
different ways. *The Merchant of Venice* said or meant
something when it left Shakespeare's hand at the end of
the sixteenth century, but today, in the light of the murder
of six million Jews in our time, it says or means something
else. One school of scholarship protests that we will get
the most out of the play if we try to see it in its Elizabethan context, but to argue that "the Elizabethans"
thought thus-and-so about Jews is scarcely convincing, for
although Shakespeare certainly was an Elizabethan, he
certainly was not a typical Elizabethan, and he need not
have held all of the commonplace views. Moreover, the
Shakespeare that interests us is the playwright, not the
Elizabethan man who (perhaps) in his routine hours held
the prejudices of the period. As Proust said, a work of
art "is the product of a different *self* from the self we
manifest in our habits, in our social life, in our vices."

Broadly, actors have given us four kinds of Shylocks:
1) a comic villain, frightening but finally ridiculous, something like a wicked stepmother or witch in a fairy tale;
2) a titanic, diabolic figure; 3) a tragic figure, a hero
brought low, a man "more sinned against than sinning" (to
use words from *King Lear*); 4) a composite figure, at
times menacing, at times pathetic, and at times absurd.
Despite much disagreement about how the role should be
interpreted, and despite the fact that Shylock appears in
only five of the play's twenty scenes, and not at all in the

fifth act, everyone agrees that the play belongs to Shylock.

Nothing is surely known about how Shylock was played
in the earliest productions. The Folio calls the play a
"Comicall Historie," but that does not prove beyond all
doubt that Shylock was portrayed comically, since a comedy was a play with a happy ending. In 1664—some
three-quarters of a century after the play was first performed—a poem was published describing Shylock:

> His beard was red, his face was made
>   Not much unlike a witch's.
> His habit was a Jewish gown
>   That would defend all weather.
> His chin turned up, his nose hung down,
>   And both ends met together.

A long-nosed, redheaded Shylock doubtless would have
been a comic figure, and quite possibly that is what Shylock was in the earliest productions, but there can be no
certainty about this.

The Merchant of Venice was done twice at court in
1605, but judging from the absence of further references,
it seems not to have been a great favorite in the first half
of the seventeenth century, and it seems not to have been
done at all in the second half. In 1701, however, George
Granville's adaptation, *The Jew of Venice*, was staged and
published in London, with the eminent Thomas Betterton
as Bassanio and Thomas Doggett as Shylock. Doggett was
known chiefly as a comic actor, so it is likely that he interpreted Shylock comically. But the comedy in the play was
somewhat reduced (two comic figures, the Gobbos, were
deleted), and Shylock's part was somewhat cut, apparently in an effort to put the emphasis on Bassanio, the
romantic hero. Other changes were the alteration of some
of Shakespeare's prose to verse, chiefly by breaking it into
lines of approximately equal length, and the addition of a
scene in Act II (the original II.i–iv were deleted) showing
Bassanio, Antonio, Shylock, and others drinking. Antonio
offers a toast to friendship. After Bassanio toasts Portia,

and Gratiano toasts all women ("be she black, or brown, or fair"), Shylock says,

> I have a mistress that outshines 'em all—
> Commanding yours—and yours though the whole sex—
> O, may her charms increase and multiply.
> My money is my mistress! Here's to
> Interest upon interest.

While there is nothing in this speech that is contrary to Shakespeare's Shylock, there is nothing in it of merit either.

Nicholas Rowe, the editor of the first critical edition of Shakespeare's plays (1709), must have had Granville's version in mind when he wrote that although he had seen *The Merchant of Venice*

> received and acted as a comedy, and the part of the Jew performed by an excellent comedian, yet I cannot but think it was designed tragically by the author. There appears in it such a deadly spirit of revenge, such a savage fierceness and fellness, and such a bloody designation of cruelty and mischief, as cannot agree either with the style or characters of comedy.

Despite Rowe's interpretation of the play, Granville's adaptation, presumably with a buffoonish Shylock, held the stage until 1741, when Charles Macklin presented at Drury Lane (and continued to present, until 1789) a Shylock who, far from being comic, was genuinely terrifying. It is said that Macklin had some difficulty persuading the management to allow him to introduce this new conception of an ominous Shylock, but Drury Lane had fallen on bad times, and apparently in desperation it took the chance, and succeeded. The performance was hailed, and Macklin's reputation was made. The mid-eighteenth-century Shylock was Macklin's, for David Garrick never played the part. It is not certainly known exactly what text Macklin used, but probably his text was close to Shakespeare's, with only minor cuts. What is certainly

known is that Macklin was immensely successful in por-
traying a monster who was to be taken seriously. For
instance, Francis Gentleman spoke of his "terrifying feroc-
ity," and Georg Lichtenberg, a German who visited
England, wrote that Macklin's Shylock

> is more than sufficient to arouse once again in the ma-
> ture man all the prejudices of his childhood against this
> race. Shylock is . . . heavy, and silent in his unfathom-
> able cunning. . . [When Shylock speaks of "three thou-
> sand ducats" he] lisps as lickerishly as if he were savoring
> the ducats and all they would buy. . . . Three such words
> uttered thus at the outset give the keynote of his whole
> character.

J. T. Kirkman, Macklin's early biographer, reported that
Macklin's Shylock exhibited "the malevolence, the villainy, the diabolical atrocity of the character." "Malevolence" seems to be the word most used, and if one gets the
impression that Macklin presented not a man but a
monster, at least the figure was to be taken seriously. In
view of later interpretations of the role, which inevitably
attempt to justify Shylock's behavior by pointing out that
he is responding to persecution, it is interesting to notice
that the behavior of Macklin's Shylock was in no way
excused. Quite the contrary: Francis Gentleman, com-
menting on the moral of the play, says that "from the
Jew's fate may be learned that persevering cruelty is very
capable of drawing ruin on itself."

Although one reads that John Philip Kemble (in the
late eighteenth century) and George Frederick Cooke (in
the first decade of the nineteenth) were impressive as Shylock, it is not until Edmund Kean interpreted the role that
one reaches something radically new. Kean, a minor actor
who had achieved some reputation in the provinces, made
his London debut on January 26, 1814, at Drury Lane.
As in Macklin's day, Drury Lane was experiencing diffi-
culties, and was therefore willing to resort to taking
chances in order to regain its popularity. Nothing prepared
the audience for what it experienced in 1814. The essayist

William Hazlitt gives us an idea of what was expected (i.e. the Macklin tradition) before Kean presented his shattering interpretation on January 26, 1814:

> When we first went to see Mr. Kean in Shylock, we expected to see a decrepit old man bent with age and ugly with mental deformity, grinning with deadly malice, with the venom of his heart congealed in the expression of his countenance, sullen, morose, gloom, inflexible, brooding over one idea, that of his hatred, and fixed on one unalterable purpose, that of his revenge.

What Kean revealed to Hazlitt was a man who,

> if he carries his revenge too far, yet he has strong grounds. . . . There is a strong, quick, and deep sense of justice mixed up with the gall and bitterness of his resentment. . . . We can hardly help sympathizing with the proud spirit, hid beneath his Jewish gaberdine, stung to madness by repeated undeserved provocations. . . .

Kean rejected what we can call the monstrous interpretation, and made Shylock more human, less mythic. He wore a black wig and black beard (perhaps unprecedented), and evoked not simply terror but pity, especially in the court scene, where his horrified look at the thought of enforced Christianity evoked sympathy in the audience. His general conception was that Shylock is not a repulsive beast but a man who has been so unjustly treated that his resentment quite understandably drives him to acts of destruction. Kean's Shylock was highly passionate, but not diabolic or monstrous or repulsive. Thus, in the scene with Tubal, in which Shylock says, "I would that my daughter were dead at my foot," according to a viewer Kean

> startled back, as with a revulsion of paternal feeling from the horrible image his avarice had conjured up, and borrowing a negative from the next inquiry ["no news of them?"], gasped an agonizing "No, no, no."

Kean made his reputation, and Shylock's, with the production in 1814. Shylock could no longer be considered a simple comic or monstrous figure. When William Charles Macready took up the role in 1823, he was often harsh, but he also conveyed a sense of restraint and sometimes even of tenderness.

The next step, soon taken, was to sentimentalize Shylock. Here is Heinrich Heine reporting on a visit to Drury Lane in 1839:

> When I saw a performance of this play at Drury Lane, a beautiful pale-faced English woman stood behind me in the box and wept profusely at the end of the fourth act, and called out repeatedly, "The poor man is wronged."
>
> . . . Thinking of those tears I must count *The Merchant of Venice* among the tragedies, although the framework of the play is ornamented with the gayest masks, satires, and love episodes, and the author's real intention was to write a comedy. Perhaps Shakespeare had in mind to create, for the entertainment of the masses, a trained werewolf, a loathsome fabulous monster thirsting for blood, and thereby losing his daughter and his ducats, and becoming a laughing stock. But the genius of the poet, the universal spirit which inspires him, is always above his individual will, and so it happened that he expressed in Shylock, in spite of all his glaring grotesqueness, the vindication of an ill-fortuned sect. . . .

Along with the elevation of Shylock to the role of sympathetic tragic hero goes the deprecation of at least some of the Christians in the play. Thus, for Heine, Lorenzo is "the receiver of stolen ducats and jewels" (true, of course), and Antonio's companions are persons who are quite as fond of money as is Shylock. In short, Heine says, "However much we must hate Shylock, we cannot blame even him if he despises those people a little." This is a far cry from, say, Francis Gentleman, who found even the jibes of Gratiano "admirably pleasant."

There was no turning back from a serious and sympathetic Shylock. In the productions of Edwin Booth, in the 1860's, when Shylock learned in the trial scene that he must become a Christian, he uttered a groan, staggered backward, gave a despairing look, and collapsed. By the way, like many others in the nineteenth century, Booth omitted the fifth act of the play, in which Shylock makes no appearance, and thus put a further emphasis on a tragic Shylock.

Henry Irving restored the fifth act in 1879, went yet further in depicting a sympathetic and tragic figure, and became the great Shylock of the second half of the century. His interpretation was enormously popular, and the production ran for two hundred and fifty nights; during his career Irving played Shylock more than a thousand times. His *Merchant of Venice* was especially famous for three things: its charming Portia (played by Ellen Terry), its illusionistic sets, and its moving Shylock. The sets, esteemed for their beauty and authenticity, included a practicable bridge over the canal. The first scene was especially rich in local color, revealing a ship moored at the right, fruit vendors, a water carrier, and Arab laborers.

Although he restored the fifth act, Irving made some serious alterations in the text. Because his sets were elaborate, it was not worth taking the time to change sets for a short scene located in Belmont that in the text appears between two scenes set in Venice, so a few scenes, such as II.ix, showing the wooing of Aragon in Belmont, were cut. A very few other scenes were cut for different reasons, probably because they included material Irving found distasteful, such as II.iii, in which Jessica says such things as "Our house is hell," and "Though I am a daughter to his blood, / I am not to his manners," and III.v, in which Jessica says, "I shall be saved by my husband. He hath made me a Christian." Other cuts, such as the great reduction in Bassanio's casket scene, also show Irving's emphasis on Shylock. And Irving cut the bawdry.

Irving's Shylock used a cane—he appeared a trifle infirm—and wore a brown gaberdine. A gray wispy beard, an Oriental shawl, and a black cap with a yellow line

across it marked him as a Jew, an outsider, but he was a
sober figure, not a grotesque one. One bit of business became especially famous. After Jessica elopes, there was the
sound of a barcarolle, some laughing maskers crossed over
the bridge, the curtain fell for a moment and then rose on
the same scene to show Shylock, lantern in hand, entering
the stage and approaching the door of his house. (Later
actors, as we shall see, amplified the business by having
Shylock enter, perceive Jessica's absence, and scream. But
Irving was content to lower the curtain as Shylock ap-
proached his empty house.) In some later scenes he
showed considerable passion, but on the whole, even
though agonized by Jessica's betrayal, Irving's Shylock
acted with considerable restraint. One reviewer, for instance, says of the passage beginning "No ill luck stirring"
(III.i.90),

> Mr. Irving . . . is now less vehement than might have
> been expected; the Jew's passion seems to have exhausted
> him. . . . He is overweighted with trouble, and the de-
> livery of the words "no ill luck stirring, but what light's
> o' my shoulders; no sighs, but o' my breathing; no tears,
> but o' my shedding," is charged with the pathos of the
> heaviest grief.

Ellen Terry reports that in the trial scene Irving for the
most part played the role of an "heroic saint," a man no
longer furious but coldly vengeful. True, in this scene he
lost some sympathy when he fawned on Portia while she
seemed to be taking his side, but his contemptuous look of
dismissal when Gratiano meanly jibed at him regained for
Shylock the audience's sympathy.

Enter William Poel, the founder of the Elizabethan
Stage Society and a man who made heroic efforts to pro-
duce Shakespeare's plays in circumstances resembling
what he took to be Elizabethan stage conditions. Poel
assumed that the Elizabethan stage was bare, and that
because it was not encumbered with sets that had to be
changed, the action could flow without interruption. Thus

the highly praised, elaborate illusionistic sets of Irving's productions were to Poel an abomination. In 1898 he staged his version of *The Merchant of Venice,* as a response to Irving's. Poel assumed that the Elizabethan Shylock was not Irving's gray-bearded dignified figure but was a red-wigged comic figure, a caricature rather like the comic stage Irishman of the late nineteenth-century English theater. The idea, again, was to get back to the original conception of the play—"the Jew that Shakespeare drew"—and not to see the play in modern terms. Poel accepted the tradition that the Elizabethan Shylock wore a red wig, and was comic in his rage, and was even comic in the trial scene, since (Poel argued) the audience's sympathy in the trial scene should be with Portia, not with Shylock. At the end of the trial scene, when Shylock departs with "I am not well" (Irving went out slowly, with dignity), Poel rushed from the stage. He explained: "Only by Shylock being 'in a great rage' as he rushes off the stage, can the audience be greatly pleased, and in a fit humor to be interested in the further doings of Portia." In 1907 Poel again staged *The Merchant of Venice,* this time seeking an even closer approximation to an Elizabethan production by not dimming the house lights and by giving the performance without intermissions. The comedy apparently was more slapstick, with Shylock something of a comic maniac seeking revenge. But the tradition of Irving was too strong to be overcome, and Poel's version was not well received. Perhaps, too, social conditions had so changed by the early twentieth century that even without Irving a strictly comic production could not be acceptable.

Although in his stagecraft Poel anticipated the future, at least insofar as modern productions are relatively swift-moving and tend to preserve Shakespeare's sequence of scenes, the spectacular and illusionistic tradition of Irving, which required deleting or rearranging short scenes, persisted for several decades, notably in productions by Herbert Beerbohm Tree and Frank Benson. Thus, although Shakespeare follows Jessica's elopement with a scene of Morocco wooing Portia in Belmont, and then

gives us Shylock reacting to the elopement, Tree in his
1908 production ran the two Venetian scenes together.
Jessica departed with her Christian friends, Shylock entered onto the stage (as Irving's Shylock had done),
knocked at the empty house, called "Jessica," raged
through the house, emerged, hurled himself to the ground,
tore his clothes, and poured ashes over his head. In a
program note Tree explained that he had improved the
play:

> In the present arrangement of the play, I have placed the
> second act entirely in the Ghetto, in order to bring the
> story of Shylock into greater cohesion. This I believe,
> has not been done before. It enables us to see much of
> the life of the Jews and the customs and manners of the
> day. For many of the details of this scene I am indebted
> to the courteous assistance of high Jewish authorities.

In speaking of "the life of the Jews and the customs and
manners of the day," Tree is referring to his much-praised
representation on the stage of Jews hanging out the
laundry, engaging in conversation, and praying.

In 1932 John Gielgud, determined to alter the by now
traditional serious Shylock, directed a performance that
treated the play as a fairy tale. Gielgud explained that he
wished "to keep the play from being the tragedy of the
Jew," and he succeeded, as he again did when he played
Shylock in 1938, but the most interesting production
between the wars was staged by the Russian émigré
Theodore Komisarjevsky, who served as guest director at
the Shakespeare Memorial Theatre in Stratford-upon-
Avon from 1932 to 1939. His first production at Stratford,
in 1932 (and repeated in the following year) was *The
Merchant of Venice*, done in a highly theatrical (which is
to say anti-illusionist) style. There was no need to group
the Belmont scenes together, as Irving, Tree, and Benson
had done, since Komisarjevsky's elaborate set for Venice
simply divided down the middle and glided off to the sides,
revealing Belmont. The play began with a masque of

Pierrots, and the commedia del l'arte motif was continued in Old Gobbo, who was the pantaloon of Italian comedy. Shylock was a comic figure, to be hooted at and dismissed from the stage without a twinge. But if the production marked the rejection of Irving's illusionism and his tragic (or sentimental?) view, it also marked the rejection of Poel's insistence that Shakespeare's plays make the most sense, and provide the most enjoyment, when they are performed on a bare stage.

The two most notable interpretations of Shylock since World War II were those by Morris Carnovsky (1957 and 1967) and Laurence Olivier (1970). In 1957, when Carnovsky performed at the American Shakespeare Festival, Stratford, Connecticut, his Shylock was a highly sympathetic figure. Carnovsky had read Harold C. Goddard's *The Meaning of Shakespeare*, which argued that Shylock proposed the bond as "a sincere wish to wipe out the past and be friends." According to Goddard, Shylock is like the lead coffin, ugly on the outside but holding something precious within. Carnovsky, in an essay of his own, published in *Tulane Drama Review* (1958) and also in an edition of the play, said that he fully believed Shylock was sincere when he said that he was proposing the forfeit of a pound of flesh merely as a "merry bond." In any case, the Goddard-Carnovsky view (and it has had considerable influence) is that the Christians are a thoroughly despicable lot. The usual charges are that Jessica is a thief and an apostate, Lorenzo is a receiver of stolen goods, and Portia and the rest of the Christians are spoiled darlings who think that money can buy anything. Only after the Christians corrupt his daughter and take from him the one creature whom he loves, does Shylock become (in Carnovsky's words) "the sad, sick, lonely wolf." The 1957 production, with Katharine Hepburn as Portia, was well received, partly because of Carnovsky's dignified acting, partly because of Hepburn's engaging manner, and partly because of a delightful fairy-tale setting. In 1967, again at Stratford in Connecticut, Carnovsky's Shylock seemed a less sympathetic figure. He was not grotesquely comic,

and certainly he was not hateful, but his emphasis on
revenge made him unsympathetic, and twice in the court
scene he became hysterical, pounding on the judge's
bench. Still, he never lost his hold on the audience, and
since Bassanio and Lorenzo were vacant fools, and Portia
a petulant young lady, he remained the most interesting
figure and really the only figure for whom the audience
could feel some respect.

In 1970 Jonathan Miller directed a production of *The
Merchant of Venice* at the National Theatre, with Laurence Oliver as a businesslike Shylock and Joan Plowright
as a rather prissy Portia. The play was set in the late
nineteenth century, with Victorian furniture for the interior scenes, and, for the exterior scenes, a square that
evoked not Venice but the financial district of London.
The trial took place in what looked like a boardroom, the
participants seated around a table. (Curiously, Olivier in
On Acting says that the idea to set the play in the nineteenth century was his, but Miller in *Subsequent Performances* says it was *his* idea.) There was little comedy,
except in the absurd Morocco and the equally absurd Aragon. This Shylock—beardless, by the way—was equipped
with a pince-nez, a frock coat, and a top hat. Only the
skullcap which he revealed when he took off his top hat
indicated that this Shylock was a Jew. For the Gentiles—
secure, elegant, arrogant young people, and silk-hatted
elders, all insiders, old boys, persons of inherited wealth
—the world was a comfortable club, a club to which Shylock (however English he sought to be) did not belong.
If one listened closely one could somehow hear that, well,
like a Disraeli or a Rothschild, he just didn't belong. Perhaps it was in the very fastidiousness of his speech that
one heard an outsider and detected disdain for the in-
group. Betrayed by his daughter, however, and pestered
by Christians, he lashed out. "Hath not a Jew eyes"
(III.i.55ff) was delivered bitingly, the speaker seeking not
to evoke pathos but to taunt. In the trial scene, dressed in
his frock coat and seated on the edge of his chair, he
attentively listened to Portia's legal reasoning, only to find

that the law is an instrument of oppression, always available to be used against outsiders. "I am content," he shouted as he left the courtroom; and then, from offstage, came the sound of someone falling, and a cry of pain. The play ended, however, on a strange and somewhat pathetic (and puzzling) note. In an added epilogue, a messenger arrives from Venice with letters for Jessica and Antonio. As they read the messages, in the distance is heard the *kaddish*, the Jewish prayer of mourning. Possibly it is Shylock wailing, or another Jew lamenting the death of Shylock. And at the very end, Jessica is alone, perhaps absorbing the fact that, like her father, she will always be an outsider.

In other postwar productions some emphasis has been put on Antonio as an outsider, and thus a parallel to Shylock. Both are merchants, are middle-aged, are pensive, and—most important—both stand apart from the general merriment. Some versions, suggesting that what makes Antonio an outsider is that he is a latent homosexual who is in love with the imperceptive Bassanio, emphasize Antonio's isolation by showing him left alone, at the end of the play, after the nicely matched couples joyfully depart without a thought for Antonio.

The BBC television version, released in the United States in 1981, did not emphasize a homosexual love, but it called attention to the superficiality and even cruelty of the supposedly sophisticated Venetian society. Portia (Gemma Jones) seemed at times a spoiled girl; by contrast, Shylock (Warren Mitchell), though scarcely amiable, seemed a man of deep integrity. Such a man, who threatens to expose the corruption beneath the superficially attractive Christian Venetian society, must be crushed if the shallow people of Venice are to preserve their pleasures.

"The Jew that Shakespeare drew" is still the subject of scholarly dispute, but the theater today gives us, in various forms, the Jew—and the Christians—that we must see in the light of the history of the twentieth century. That is, our view is, quite properly, conditioned at least as much by Nazi Germany as it is by Renaissance England.

Suggested References

The number of possible references is vast and grows alarmingly. (The *Shakespeare Quarterly* devotes one issue each year to a list of the previous year's work, and *Shakespeare Survey* —an annual publication—includes a substantial review of recent scholarship, as well as an occasional essay surveying a few decades of scholarship on a chosen topic.) Though no works are indispensable, those listed below have been found helpful.

1. Shakespeare's Times

Byrne, M. St. Clare. *Elizabethan Life in Town and Country*. Rev. ed. New York: Barnes & Noble, 1961. Chapters on manners, beliefs, education, etc., with illustrations.

Joseph, B. L. *Shakespeare's Eden: The Commonwealth of England, 1558–1629*. New York: Barnes and Noble, 1971. An account of the social, political, economic, and cultural life of England.

Schoenbaum, S. *Shakespeare: The Globe and the World*. New York: Oxford University Press, 1979. A readable, handsomely illustrated book on the world of the Elizabethans.

Shakespeare's England. 2 vols. London: The Oxford University Press, 1916. A large collection of scholarly essays on a wide variety of topics (e.g., astrology, costume, gardening, horsemanship), with special attention to Shakespeare's references to these topics.

Stone, Lawrence. *The Crisis of the Aristocracy, 1558–1641*, abridged edition. London: Oxford University Press, 1967.

2. Shakespeare

Barnet, Sylvan. *A Short Guide to Shakespeare*. New York: Harcourt Brace Jovanovich, 1974. An introduction to all of the works and to the dramatic traditions behind them.

Bentley, Gerald E. *Shakespeare: A Biographical Handbook*. New Haven, Conn.: Yale University Press, 1961. The facts about Shakespeare, with virtually no conjecture intermingled.

Bush, Geoffrey. *Shakespeare and the Natural Condition*. Cambridge, Mass.: Harvard University Press, 1956. A short, sensitive account of Shakespeare's view of "Nature," touching most of the works.

Chambers, E. K. *William Shakespeare: A Study of Facts and Problems*. 2 vols. London: Oxford University Press, 1930. An invaluable, detailed reference work; not for the casual reader.

Chute, Marchette. *Shakespeare of London*. New York: Dutton, 1949. A readable biography fused with portraits of Stratford and London life.

Clemen, Wolfgang H. *The Development of Shakespeare's Imagery*. Cambridge, Mass.: Harvard University Press, 1951. (Originally published in German, 1936.) A temperate account of a subject often abused.

Granville-Barker, Harley. *Prefaces to Shakespeare*. 2 vols. Princeton, N.J.: Princeton University Press, 1946–47. Essays on ten plays by a scholarly man of the theater.

Harbage, Alfred. *As They Liked It*. New York: Macmillan, 1947. A long, sensitive essay on Shakespeare, morality, and the audience's expectations.

Kernan, Alvin B., ed. *Modern Shakespearean Criticism: Essays on Style, Dramaturgy, and the Major Plays*. New York: Harcourt Brace Jovanovich, 1970. A collection of major formalist criticism.

———. "The Plays and the Playwrights." In *The Revels History of Drama in English*, general editors Clifford Leech and T. W. Craik. Vol. III. London: Methuen, 1975. A book-length essay surveying Elizabethan drama with substantial discussions of Shakespeare's plays.

Schoenbaum, S. *Shakespeare's Lives*. Oxford: Clarendon Press, 1970. A review of the evidence, and an examination of many biographies, including those by Baconians and other heretics.

———. *William Shakespeare: A Compact Documentary Life*. New York: Oxford University Press, 1977. A readable presentation of all that the documents tell us about Shakespeare.

Traversi, D. A. *An Approach to Shakespeare*. 3rd rev. ed. 2 vols. New York: Doubleday, 1968–69. An analysis of the plays beginning with words, images, and themes, rather than with characters.

Van Doren, Mark. *Shakespeare*. New York: Holt, 1939. Brief, perceptive readings of all the plays.

3. Shakespeare's Theater

Beckerman, Bernard. *Shakespeare at the Globe, 1599–1609*. New York: Macmillan, 1962. On the playhouse and on Elizabethan dramaturgy, acting, and staging.

Chambers, E. K. *The Elizabethan Stage*. 4 vols. New York: Oxford University Press, 1945. A major reference work on theaters, theatrical companies, and staging at court.

Cook, Ann Jennalie. *The Privileged Playgoers of Shakespeare's London, 1576–1642*. Princeton, N.J.: Princeton University Press, 1981. Sees Shakespeare's audience as more middle-class and more intellectual than Harbage (below) does.

Gurr, Andrew. *The Shakespearean Stage: 1574–1642*. 2nd edition. Cambridge: Cambridge University Press, 1980. On the acting companies, the actors, the playhouses, the stages, and the audiences.

Harbage, Alfred. *Shakespeare's Audience*. New York: Columbia University Press, 1941. A study of the size and nature of the theatrical public, emphasizing its representativeness.

Hodges, C. Walter. *The Globe Restored*. London: Ernest Benn, 1953. A well-illustrated and readable attempt to reconstruct the Globe Theatre.

Hosley, Richard. "The Playhouses." In *The Revels History of Drama in English*, general editors Clifford Leech and T. W. Craik. Vol. III. London: Methuen, 1975. An essay of one hundred pages on the physical aspects of the playhouses.

Kernodle, George R. *From Art to Theatre: Form and Convention in the Renaissance*. Chicago: University of Chicago Press, 1944. Pioneering and stimulating work on the symbolic and cultural meanings of theater construction.

Nagler, A. M. *Shakespeare's Stage*. Trans. by Ralph Manheim. New Haven, Conn.: Yale University Press, 1958. A very brief introduction to the physical aspects of the playhouse.

Slater, Ann Pasternak. *Shakespeare the Director*. Totowa, N.J.: Barnes & Noble, 1982. An analysis of theatrical effects (e.g., kissing, kneeling) in stage directions and dialogue.

Thomson, Peter. *Shakespeare's Theatre*. London: Routledge & Kegan Paul, 1983. A discussion of how plays were staged in Shakespeare's time.

4. Miscellaneous Reference Works

Abbott, E. A. *A Shakespearean Grammar*. New Edition. New York: Macmillan, 1877. An examination of differences between Elizabethan and modern grammar.

Bevington, David. *Shakespeare*. Arlington Heights, Ill.: A. H. M. Publishing, 1978. A short guide to hundreds of important writings on the works.

Bullough, Geoffrey. *Narrative and Dramatic Sources of Shakespeare*. 8 vols. New York: Columbia University Press, 1957–75. A collection of many of the books Shakespeare drew upon, with judicious comments.

Campbell, Oscar James, and Edward G. Quinn. *The Reader's Encyclopedia of Shakespeare*. New York: Crowell, 1966. More than 2,600 entries, from a few sentences to a few pages, on everything related to Shakespeare.

Greg, W. W. *The Shakespeare First Folio*. New York: Oxford University Press, 1955. A detailed yet readable history of the first collection (1623) of Shakespeare's plays.

Kökeritz, Helge. *Shakespeare's Names*. New Haven, Conn.: Yale University Press, 1959. A guide to the pronunciation of some 1,800 names appearing in Shakespeare.

———. *Shakespeare's Pronunciation*. New Haven, Conn.: Yale University Press, 1953. Contains much information about puns and rhymes.

Muir, Kenneth. *The Sources of Shakespeare's Plays*. New Haven, Conn.: Yale University Press, 1978. An account of Shakespeare's use of his reading.

The Norton Facsimile: The First Folio of Shakespeare. Prepared by Charlton Hinman. New York: Norton, 1968. A handsome and accurate facsimile of the first collection (1623) of Shakespeare's plays.

Onions, C. T. *A Shakespeare Glossary*. 2d ed., rev., with en-

larged addenda. London: Oxford University Press, 1953.
Definitions of words (or senses of words) now obsolete.

Partridge, Eric. *Shakespeare's Bawdy*. Rev. ed. New York:
Dutton; London: Routledge & Kegan Paul, 1955. A glossary of bawdy words and phrases.

Shakespeare Quarterly. See headnote to Suggested References.

Shakespeare Survey. See headnote to Suggested References.

Shakespeare's Plays in Quarto. A Facsimile Edition. Ed.
Michael J. B. Allen and Kenneth Muir. Berkeley, Calif.:
University of California Press, 1981. A book of nine hundred pages, containing facsimiles of twenty-two of the
quarto editions of Shakespeare's plays. An invaluable com-
plement to *The Norton Facsimile: The First Folio of Shakespeare* (see above).

Smith, Gordon Ross. *A Classified Shakespeare Bibliography
1936–1958*. University Park, Pa.: Pennsylvania State University Press, 1963. A list of some 20,000 items on Shakespeare.

Spevack, Marvin. *The Harvard Concordance to Shakespeare*.
Cambridge, Mass.: Harvard University Press, 1973. An
index to Shakespeare's words.

Wells, Stanley, ed. *Shakespeare: Select Bibliographies*. London: Oxford University Press, 1973. Seventeen essays surveying scholarship and criticism of Shakespeare's life, work,
and theater.

5. *The Merchant of Venice*

Barber, C. L. *Shakespeare's Festive Comedy*. Princeton, N.J.:
Princeton University Press, 1959.

Barnet, Sylvan, ed. *Twentieth Century Interpretations of "The
Merchant of Venice."* Englewood Cliffs, N.J.: Prentice-Hall,
1970.

———. "Prodigality and Time in *The Merchant of Venice*,"
PMLA, 87 (1972), 26–30.

Brown, John Russell, ed. *The Arden Shakespeare: The Merchant of Venice*, 7th rev. ed. London: Methuen, 1955.

———. "The Realization of Shylock: A Theatrical Criticism."
In *Stratford-upon-Avon Studies 3: Early Shakespeare*, eds.
John Russell Brown and Bernard Harris. London: Edward
Arnold, 1961. 187–209.

Geary, Keith. "The Nature of Portia's Victory: Turning to Men in *The Merchant of Venice*," *Shakespeare Survey,* 37 (1984), 55–68.

Jordan, William Chester. "Approaches to the Court Scene in *The Merchant of Venice*," *Shakespeare Quarterly,* 33 (1982), 49–59.

Leggatt, Alexander. *Shakespeare's Comedy of Love.* London: Methuen, 1974. Part of the material is reproduced above.

Nevo, Ruth. *Comic Transformations in Shakespeare.* London: Methuen, 1980.

Novy, Marianne. *Love's Argument: Gender Relations in Shakespeare.* Chapel Hill, N.C.: University of North Carolina Press, 1984.

Rabkin, Norman. *Shakespeare and the Problem of Meaning.* Chicago: University of Chicago Press, 1980.

Slights, Camille. "In Defense of Jessica," *Shakespeare Quarterly* 31 (1980), 357–68.

C

SIGNET CLASSICS for Your Library

BRITISH CLASSICS

(0451)

☐ **LORD JIM** by Joseph Conrad.   (522346—$2.25)

☐ **NOSTROMO** by Joseph Conrad. Foreword by F.R. Leavis.
(523474—$4.95)

☐ **HEART OF DARKNESS** and **THE SECRET SHARER** by Joseph Conrad. Introduction by Albert J. Guerard.   (523210—$2.95)

☐ **FAR FROM THE MADDENING CROWD** by Thomas Hardy. Afterword by James Wright Macalester.   (523601—$3.95)

☐ **JUDE THE OBSCURE** by Thomas Hardy. Foreword by A. Alvarez.
(523709—$3.95)

☐ **THE MAYOR OF CASTERBRIDGE** by Thomas Hardy. Afterword by Walter Allen.   (525191—$2.95)

☐ **THE RETURN OF THE NATIVE** by Thomas Hardy.   (524713—$2.95)

☐ **TESS OF THE D'URBERVILLES** by Thomas Hardy. Afterword by Donald Hall.   (525469—$3.50)

☐ **KIM** by Rudyard Kipling. Afterword by Raymond Carney.
(525493—$2.50)

☐ **CAPTAINS COURAGEOUS** by Rudyard Kipling. Afterword by C.A. Bodelsen.
(523814—$2.25)

☐ **THE JUNGLE BOOKS** by Rudyard Kipling. Afterword by Marcus Cunliffe.
(523407—$3.95)

☐ **JUST SO STORIES** by Rudyard Kipling.   (524330—$3.50)

Prices slightly higher in Canada.